Making Perfect Takeoffs in Light Airplanes

Making Perfect

Takeoffs

in Light Airplanes

RON FOWLER

IOWA STATE UNIVERSITY PRESS

A M E S

This book is for Bet, Karen, and Ben

Ron Fowler is a flight instructor and teaches aviation courses at Valencia Community College, Orlando, Florida, where he is also director of aviation curriculum. He is the author of *Making Perfect Landings in Light Airplanes* (Iowa State University Press), *Flying the Commercial Flight Test* (Macmillan), *Preflight Planning* (Macmillan), and *Flying Precision Maneuvers in Light Airplanes* (Delacorte Press).

Illustrations by **Jan Avis**
Photographs by **John Tate**

© 1991 Iowa State University Press, Ames, Iowa 50010
All rights reserved

The excerpt from Ernest K. Gann, *Fate Is the Hunter,* Simon and Schuster, 1961, is reprinted with permission from Simon and Schuster. The excerpt from Richard Bach, *A Gift of Wings,* Delacorte Press, 1974, is reprinted with permission from Richard Bach. The excerpt from Beryl Markham, *West with the Night,* North Point Press, 1983, copyright © 1984 by Beryl Markham, is reprinted with permission from North Point Press.

Authorization to photocopy items for internal or personal use, or the internal or personal use of specific clients, is granted by Iowa State University Press, provided that the base fee of $.10 per copy is paid directly to the Copyright Clearance Center, 27 Congress Street, Salem, MA 01970. For those organizations that have been granted a photocopy license by CCC, a separate system of payments has been arranged. The fee code for users of the Transactional Reporting Service is 0-8138-0949-5/91 $.10.

⊗ Printed on acid-free paper in the United States of America

First edition, 1991

Library of Congress Cataloging-in-Publication Data
Fowler, Ron
    Making perfect takeoffs in light airplanes / Ron Fowler.—1st ed.
        p.   cm.
    Includes bibliographical references and index.
    ISBN 0-8138-0949-5 (alk. paper)
    1. Airplanes—Take-off. 2. Private flying. I. Title.
TL711.T3F68   1991
629.132′5217—dc20   91-15181

Contents

Preface, vii

1. Basic Considerations of a Normal Takeoff, 3

2. Short-Field Takeoffs, 45

3. Soft-Field Takeoffs, 70

4. Critical Takeoff Situations, 79

5. Night Takeoffs, 93

6. Tailwheel Takeoffs, 111

7. Cardinal Rules for Perfect Takeoffs, 122

Epilogue, 129

Appendix: *Some Rules of Thumb Concerning Takeoffs,* 131

Suggested Reading, 135

Index, 137

Preface

It was truly one of the worst flights I've ever flown. Years have passed and it is still too easy to remember. The pilot had had a flying accident several weeks prior—pilot error on takeoff that had cost an airplane and a few scrapes and bruises. Now, the FAA required that he obtain recurrent training to bring his pilot skills back to par before again acting as pilot in command. He called on a Saturday afternoon to ask if I would drive out to the small, rural field and begin the training. Sure, I'd said.

The runway concerned me the moment I stepped from the car and saw it—about 50/50 Bahia grass and soft, white ·Florida sand. And short, very short indeed. But the pilot's plane was born of short strips—a just-purchased, restored, vintage two-seat tailwheeler of the forties. The little cream-and-yellow ship was one of my favorite models, one in which I had flown many past hours of pleasure. But I had an uneasy feeling.

The departure end of the strip worried me. The runway ended at a grove of rotund, squat orange trees. Draped high above these were the wires of a power line. Yet, I knew full well that two generations of pilots had enjoyed the airport. (And *that* is very seductive erroneous reasoning.)

We planned the takeoff carefully. Weight and balance, take-off charted against the summer heat and turf surface, plus a bit extra for the patches of soft sand and the kids at home. Then, a nose-to-aluminum preflight inspection and a full-power run-up, and yet the unease presisted.

After everything checked out, the pilot and I walked to the strip's far end and paced off the climb distance we would need and marked our "abort point" with a notebook page pinned to the turf with a stick. Finally, we manually backed the plane a few extra yards to snug the tail against the runway threshold.

I remember taking a moment's pause with one foot on the ground, the other on the spud. The plane was trying to tell me something, something seen by my eye but not yet seen by my mind. But I could not make out its whispered message, lost amid the loud buzz of the afternoon cicadas. I shrugged, went on superalert, and climbed aboard.

We were ready for takeoff.

The pilot pressed in full throttle and a smidge of right rudder to counter the P factor and the slipstream effect. Normal acceleration brought the tail up right on schedule. The sturdy steel-spring gear smoothed out bumps as we gained momentum behind the singing Continental. We could see the white patch of our abort marker ahead when the little ship traded its Earthbound clamor for its airborne life.

But something was wrong!

Even as the wheels cleared, my right hand was sliding toward the yoke. And even as my left hand replaced that of the pilot's on the throttle, the plane's softly spoken message came through 5 × 5.

We were not climbing.

Those wires ahead remained virtually motionless across the windscreen. I pinned the nose at best angle of climb speed. The wires started oozing downward, but even so I could see we were not going to clear them. I could not fly beneath them either. Those as-yet-unfruited orange trees prevented that. Neither could I turn away. Not only would the turn cost the meager rate of climb, but my mind's eye saw that power line stretching to the horizon's curvature. Any attempt to land on the remaining runway would now be disaster—I had waited too long.

We three—the pilot, the plane, and myself—flew toward

those wires, climbing with all the alacrity of a rusty jackscrew. I was deep into wondering what to do next, adrenaline squirting from both ears, when the wires arrived.

There was only one choice open. At the last moment I hiked the nose upward toward the stall. In the long run that would cost climb, but there *was* no long run. I hoped for a momentary, pathetic zoom of 4 or 5 feet—and got it.

We headed for the municipal airport of long runways and landed to sort things out. The reason for the little ship's hazardous takeoff performance was obvious. It had been obvious even as I preflighted, but I had not taken notice. During restoration the wing's fabric had been replaced with aluminum. The plane still *looked* the same, but extra weight and a possible change in airfoil shape drastically altered its takeoff ability. Altered enough, certainly, to make the manufacturer's takeoff performance chart pure fiction.

I was reminded once more that takeoff is the most critical phase of flight.

One only need look at the statistics to confirm the truth of this. For as many years as I can remember, the FAA has listed takeoffs and landings as the times and places for the overwhelming majority of flying accidents. And of these two phases, the takeoff produces the greater accident frequency. Yet, as pilots, we often think of the landing as the more critical of the two. As students we looked toward landings as the culmination of our piloting expertise. Then, as rated pilots, we work with concentration to deliver a smooth-as-Aeroshell landing to our passengers—and often perform the takeoff with little care about precision and planning. Yet those statistics are there, year after year, telling us, Beware of the takeoff.

There are some basic reasons, two in fact, that make a takeoff more critical than a landing.

Reason 1: When landing, the haven of safety lies down *there; when taking off, the haven resides* up *there.*
Examples of this reason are easy to find. There are factors

surrounding both maneuvers that impede a takeoff far more than they do a landing. Simple gravity for one. In a landing we are coming down anyway. (In all of recorded aviation history, we haven't yet gotten a plane stuck up there.) But on takeoff gravity fights every inch of altitude. We had better be behind an optimally performing engine clawing its way through an acceptable density altitude.

Another example of reason number one at play? Inertia. It is usually easier to stop something than it is to keep it going. In a landing, we know that a stop concludes the maneuver. We count on it, and the forces at play generally assist us in this effort. But on a takeoff there *is* no conclusion. We *must* keep the thing under way. We cannot take a breather any more than we could clear a mud puddle with two steps. Yet many of the forces that may help bring a landing plane to rest resist our attempts to get it into the air and keep it there. The runway condition or underinflated tires, for example, that drag our landing plane to an early stop make a departing plane hug the ground with all the cling of an egg dropped onto the kitchen floor.

There are examples aplenty that make the up-there/down-there concept of safe haven apply differently to takeoffs than to landings. Each example reminds us once more that humans were not intended to fly.

Reason 2: A tried pilot, a true airplane.

A landing usually has a pilot aboard with very recent flight experience, an hour or so at the controls. But let's face it. We don't fly as often as we would like. The pilot at the helm on takeoff may not have touched those controls in a week, month, or (gulp!) several months.

The plane is in much the same situation. That plane on landing has already proven itself a true ship for the past hour or so of flying time. But at takeoff it is a different matter altogether. The plane is unproven. Will it perform? Does it have the capability to meet the situation at hand? Only a totally aware pilot can tell for sure.

While on this topic of total awareness, let me turn back to that recurrent-training flight for my pilot friend. Why did that near-accident happen? I would like to excuse it by saying I was a relatively inexperienced flight instructor at the time. But that simply won't wash. Even inexperienced pilots could have made themselves aware of the potential hazard before rather than after the fact. Let's look at some warnings that became part of my awareness *after* lift-off.

1. The wing had been metalized.
2. The plane was purchased—(choke!) undemonstrated—from a dealer at a nearby airport with long runways.
3. The dealer's pilot had delivered the plane to my friend's short strip.
4. The plane had not flown since that delivery flight.

Had I made myself aware of the significances that lay behind these facts, I would have made four preflight decisions to stack the deck in my favor.

1. I would have delayed the flight until I had cooler temperatures and a better headwind.
2. I would have delayed the flight until the wind favored the other end of the runway. There were no obstacles in that direction. Indeed, there was even a tomato field straight ahead that would have provided a safe, if somewhat juicy, landing.
3. I would have taken off with half tanks and without my friend's weight aboard.
4. I would have then flown to a longer runway for subsequent flights until we better knew that airplane.

But I did none of these things. Inexperience was no excuse; a lack of total awareness was the reason.

Total awareness means never being caught by surprise in the cockpit. It is a concept that many pilots hear about but few experience. The majority of pilots who never attain total awareness let it elude them simply because they do not understand its simplicity. They feel that it is only "theory stuff." Yet it is a real and very visible tool, a pilot's sixth sense that elevates the professional flyer above the unprofessional. (And by "professional" I do not mean a pilot who flies for hire or one who has accumulated thousands of hours aloft. I mean a pilot determined to deliver the very best that pilot and plane, as a team, can give.)

This book, then, is written with the desire to help pilots develop a total awareness—the forces that surround and influence, the procedures to use, the pitfalls to avoid—in that most critical phase of flight, making a perfect takeoff.

Plane and sky grant no special consideration. Whether we walk the Earth as good or bad, wise or foolish, poor or rich makes no difference. When we enter the cockpit we leave behind our Earthbound differences. We touch the controls as one—a pilot. If we are competent, our flying will probably succeed. And if we are incompetent, our flying will probably fail.

—*Basic truth of flying*

CHAPTER ONE

Basic Considerations
of a Normal Takeoff

All too often many pilots think of their takeoff as only those few seconds between pushing the throttle forward and lifting the wheels from the runway. This is erroneous thinking that practically guarantees a takeoff lacking in concentration. As an example of what I mean, consider the pro golfer readying for a drive down the fairway. That pro does not consider the swing and millisecond of ball contact as the sum total of the drive. Rather, as integral parts of the effort, the golfer includes those moments spent in addressing the ball before the strike and the follow-through afterward. The pro understands the need for that brief moment before the swing and uses it to bring concentration into sharp focus on the job at hand and to personally synchronize with ball and club. The pro knows too that a follow-through is needed to prevent a premature break in concentration during that critical instant of truth that delivers the drive straight down the fairway.

So it is with takeoffs. Your takeoff will have its address, delivery, and follow-through. You need to include those steps that put you in tune with the plane and the sky. Steps that bring focus and ensure concentration. Think then, of your takeoff as a series of steps that begin long before the plane is astride the center line and continue well after the wheels lift off. Perform each step with precision, each step having its own goal to achieve.

1. Starting the engine.
2. Taxiing to the runway.
3. Performing the pretakeoff checks.
4. Taking the runway.
5. Making the takeoff run.
6. Lifting off.
7. Flying the initial climbout.
8. Leaving the pattern.
9. Climbing to cruise altitude.
10. Leveling to cruise.

Starting the Engine

Starting an aircraft engine is no trivial matter and cannot be handled in a cavalier manner. There is too much at stake for that. The two prime considerations of an engine-starting procedure must be

1. The safety of those in and around the aircraft.
2. The protection of the plane's power plant and airframe accessories.

Use a checklist to achieve a professional and precise engine-start procedure. Here are some items that should be included in a typical light-plane engine-starting checklist.

1. Seat belt and harness: fastened.
2. Seat position: locked in track.
3. Landing-gear handle or switch: down and locked.
4. Fuel-tank selector: freedom of movement; proper tank.
5. Cowl flaps: open.
6. Carburetor heat: closed.
7. Propeller: set for high rpm.
8. Avionics and electrical equipment: off.
9. Fuel mixture: full rich or as required.
10. Throttle: start position.

11. Primer pump: prime engine.
12. Propeller area: Clear!
13. Electrical master switch: on.
14. Auxiliary electric fuel pump: on.
15. Brakes: hold or set.
16. Magnetos: on.
17. Start engine: avoid prolonged cranking.
18. Throttle: adjust for warm-up (1000–1200 rpm).
19. Oil pressure: normal within 30 seconds.
20. Ammeter: normal.

Let's take a moment to discuss some of the *significances* that lie behind each of these checklist items.

SEAT BELT AND HARNESS: FASTENED. It is important that every occupant be belted and harnessed before taxi begins. A collision with converging taxiing aircraft is just as devastating as an auto accident.

Federal Aviation Regulations (FARs) require the pilot to instruct passengers in the fastening and unfastening of belt and harness. This is important for safety. Different belts buckle differently. It is conceivable that a situation could occur wherein split seconds count in unbuckling and evacuating the aircraft. Make this instruction an integral part of checklist item number one.

SEAT POSITION: LOCKED IN TRACK. After you have adjusted your seat position, wiggle your rump to make certain that the seat is locked on its track. A pilot who slides out of reach of the rudder pedals at rotation is bound to attract the attention of all on board. (A sliding seat may present the pilot with another distraction. If the front-seat passenger's seat cuts loose, that passenger may try to stem the slide by grabbing the yoke. Be ready.)

Improper seat position is often the reason for erratic rudder control. Many pilots sit with the seat entirely too close to the controls. Adjust the seat so that near-full leg extension still allows firm brake pressure with full rudder deflection.

LANDING GEAR: DOWN AND LOCKED. Make certain that the landing-gear handle or switch is in the down-and-locked position. It is very possible for a boarding passenger to accidentally flip an electrical switch to the "retract" position. Then when the master switch is thrown, surprises may occur. Oh, I know that gears may be equipped with a "squat" switch to keep the wheels from coming up when the weight of the aircraft rests on the gear. But these sensitive switches are checked only once a year.

FUEL-TANK SELECTOR: FREEDOM OF MOVEMENT; PROPER TANK. Rotate the fuel-selector handle through its full travel before positioning it to the takeoff tank. This is to make sure you can switch to the next tank when the time comes. Handles do become stuck, and a boarding passenger can step on the thing and bend it. I've even had handles come off when I've turned them.

Consult your aircraft manual to determine the proper takeoff tank. Most light-plane manuals suggest "fullest tank," but a few specify a certain fuel cell.

Here is a rule of thumb to follow: never take off with less than one-quarter capacity showing on the gauges, not even for a quick turn about the pattern. Even though you may anticipate a flight of only a few minutes, a runway situation, for example, or an aircraft discrepancy aloft may prolong your need to stay airborne.

COWL FLAPS: OPEN. If you are flying a plane with cowl flaps, for proper cooling they should be open during taxi, run-up, and climb (Fig. 1–1). Now is the time to open them, lest you forget.

CARBURETOR HEAT: CLOSED. Your carburetor heat flow should be closed on the ground for two reasons. First, the air passing through the heater to the carburetor is unfiltered, and you do not want to pass the prop-stirred grit into the engine. Second, hot air from the heater further enriches the fuel mixture. You are already operating on "full rich" and any excess is more than we should ask the engine to digest.

1.1. Unless the conditions are extremely cold, cowl flaps should be open during ground operations and climb.

PROPELLER: SET FOR HIGH RPM. Engines equipped with constant-speed props should be cranked with the propeller set for high rpm. This fine pitch reduces the prop's drag through the air as it moves, which reduces battery drain.

AVIONICS AND ELECTRICAL EQUIPMENT: OFF. Radios can suffer damage due to surges when cranking. Some electrical accessories draw enough current to drain a battery that is busy turning a starter. Avionics and electrical equipment should be turned off for starting. Should you kill the battery, *do not attempt to start the engine by hand propping unless you have had instruction in the procedure.* To do so is to invite a particularly nasty accident.

FUEL MIXTURE: FULL RICH OR AS REQUIRED. Most aircraft manuals have you using a rich mixture to ensure a quicker start, which saves battery life. Some aircraft, however, need a reduced or closed mixture to achieve the same result. Consult the airplane manual—don't just make up your own procedure.

THROTTLE: START POSITION. Again, the aircraft manual states the proper throttle position for engine start. Different makes and models vary on the subject. If the engine fails to fire readily by use of the manual's starting procedure, it is often a signal that the carburetion or ignition system needs attention.

Avoid starting the engine with excess throttle. High rpm's during that moment after starting adds unwarranted wear to an engine that has not yet coated its internal parts with oil. Also, be aware of what lies in the line of your propwash. A blast of dust and grit aimed toward the maintenance hangar, for instance, is bound to stir an acquaintance with the mechanic, especially if an engine lies open on the bench or a new paint job is drying.

PRIMER PUMP: PRIME ENGINE. The primer pump delivers a squirt of fuel directly into the engine's cylinders. A properly primed engine cranks quickly and saves wear to the battery and starter. When starting the engine, use the manual-approved method of priming; use either the primer pump or the auxiliary fuel pump. Don't, however, attempt to prime by pumping the throttle. This method is apt to flood the carburetor with raw gasoline. Then, a backfire on starting can produce a fire. Should you ever experience a carburetor fire, keep cranking that engine. With luck, the fire will be sucked into the cylinders. If cranking for several seconds does not put out the fire, get yourself and the passengers out of the plane. If the fire *does* extinguish, shut down and inspect for damage.

PROPELLER AREA: CLEAR! Make sure the propeller area is clear of pedestrians before cranking the engine. After you have yelled, Clear! with drill-sergeant enthusiasm, look ahead, left and right, and to the rear for nonpilots who might think you are only anouncing a cloudless sky. A methodical visual check also prevents the shortest lapsed time in all of flying, those microseconds that many pilots squeeze between the shout of warning and the swinging of the blades.

The plane is often parked near the Fixed Base Operator's (FBO) door, in an area of heavy foot traffic. It's a dangerous place for a running engine. Stay superalert for nonpilots, especially children. They will simply be unaware of that invisible propeller arc. Should you see someone approaching your plane, stop the engine. Don't do it in the ordinary manner of closing the fuel-mixture control to run the carburetor dry—that takes too long. Simply kill the mags for a fast stop.

ELECTRICAL MASTER SWITCH: ON. Throwing the master switch in an airplane performs the same function as the first "notch" in your automobile's ignition switch; it activates the electrical system. Many light planes have a split-type switch with halves labeled "alternator" and "battery" (Fig. 1.2). Normally both halves are used simultaneously. The alternator side of the switch may be turned off to remove the alternator from the electrical system while the circuit continues to function. This is done when starting the engine with external power in order to protect the alternator from possible power surge or improper hookup of the jumper cable.

1.2. Split-type master switches allow the pilot to remove the alternator from the electrical system.

AUXILIARY ELECTRIC FUEL PUMP: ON. The auxiliary electric fuel
pump is there to deliver fuel to the engine, should the engine-
driven fuel pump fail in flight. Most aircraft equipped with such a
pump ask the pilot to use it during engine start to ensure a consistent fuel flow before the engine actually fires. It is also our only
chance to observe if it really works.

Once the engine starts, however, you want to turn off the
auxiliary pump. This move is needed to make sure the engine-
driven pump is doing *its* job.

Some aircraft, particularly those with fuel-injection systems,
use the auxiliary fuel pump in lieu of a primer pump. Again, use it
in accordance with the aircraft's manual.

BRAKES: HOLD OR SET. Hold or set the brakes to prevent the
plane from jumping ahead at engine start. It's a toss-up
whether to hold with toe brakes or to set the hand brake. Each has
its hazard. When holding the brakes with your toes, for instance, a
cockpit distraction may cause you to inadvertently release pressure.
Hand brakes, however, sometimes jump out of the locked position.
So do whichever you think is best but be alert to the shortcomings.

MAGNETOS: ON. Most light aircraft are designed to start with
"both" mags engaged. A few airplanes (those with impulse
starting), however, are designed to start on the "left" magneto only.
Refer to your aircraft's manual to know for sure.

START ENGINE: AVOID PROLONGED CRANKING. If the engine
is difficult to start, avoid prolonged cranking; the starter armature will overheat and may cause permanent damage. If prolonged cranking becomes necessary, allow the starter 1 minute of
cooling between each 20-second interval of cranking. And remember: if the recommended starting procedure does not fire the engine
in due time, you are getting a strong warning that the engine may
require attention.

THROTTLE: ADJUST FOR WARM-UP. An aircraft engine must be warmed up at low rpm's (1000–1200 rpm). Most engine wear occurs during the first moments of operation before the engine is warm. Avoid using operating power during this critical time. The engine is warm and ready for normal operating power when the application of throttle does not cause engine "hesitation," or when the oil-temperature needle climbs to the green arc.

OIL PRESSURE: NORMAL WITHIN 30 SECONDS. Under normal circumstances, the oil pressure should reach the operating range on the gauge within several seconds. If a malfunction of the system, or extremely cold weather, does not allow it to do so within 30 seconds of engine start, shut down to prevent irreversible damage to the engine.

Very cold temperature is the most common culprit of low oil pressure when starting an engine. The oil within the sump has congealed into a lump of lard that cannot get to the engine. In these instances preheating of the engine may be necessary. (Be aware that congealed oil within the system may give a false indication of pressure for a few seconds after cranking, but it will quickly fall to zero as any residual oil is pumped back into the sump.)

AMMETER: NORMAL. The ammeter indicates the condition of the electrical circuits' recharge system. Ammeters display their message in one of two fashions. With some, either a charge or discharge condition is shown. A reading of zero shortly after the engine fires means normal charging. Other ammeters indicate the alternator output. With these, a zero reading indicates a loss of alternator output. To verify working order for either type of instrument, momentarily turn on the landing light and look for a normal small movement of the needle.

Should the "over-voltage" warning light come on, switch off both halves of the master switch for 10 seconds to allow the alternator to reset. If the over-voltage condition does not reoccur when the master switch is again thrown, continue. If, however, the over-voltage condition again activates the warning light, a malfunction is likely.

There is a lot to do in starting an aircraft engine, and in the interests of safety and protection of the equipment, it cannot be done in a haphazard manner. From the moment I'm seated, it takes about 4 minutes to work my way through the engine-starting checklist. This time is well spent. Meticulously performed, starting the engine is a good first step that puts you in tune with your aircraft and fully prepares you for taxiing.

Taxiing to the Runway

After the engine has warmed to operating temperature, begin taxiing, the second step of your takeoff sequence. Taxi with two golden rules firmly in mind.

1. Remain cautious of other aircraft.
2. Avoid abrupt actions with power, brakes, and steering.

The simple fact is that other pilots may not be looking. Those same pilots who, while aloft, spot planes with the enthusiasm of a B-17 tailgunner often do not look where they are taxiing. Taxi defensively. Give a wide berth to any plane, moving or not, whose pilot is in the cockpit. Expect parked pilots to fire up and jump ahead without looking. Assume that head-on traffic is going to squeeze you off into the grass and expect converging planes to hold an intercept course. Stay alert and keep in mind that all those other planes are maintaining your exact altitude.

All of this means that you need to focus your attention on the task at hand. When taxiing keep your eyes busy outside the cockpit. As much as possible, while the plane is moving avoid noncritical cockpit tasks such as sorting charts, setting up the navaids, or copying clearances. Strongly discourage conversation from a passenger. Rather, take that time to allow your thinking to synchronize more and more with the plane that you will soon launch.

Grade your taxiing by the degree of smoothness you give to the ride. Begin this effort right from the moment you advance the throttle to start rolling. Avoid a jackrabbit start. Rather than beginning with a blast of power, squeeze in 50 rpm increments of power until you get breakaway. Once rolling, throttle back to a power that gives a slow taxi.

Taxi slowly. Those little bitty wheels do not give much stability at high taxi speeds. (Imagine how secure you would feel in downtown traffic if your car's tires were the same size.) Once under way, plan ahead to maintain a constant slow speed. If, for example, you see that an upcoming turn will put the wind at your tail, be prepared to reduce throttle to keep the speed constant. Or, if you see an upgrade ahead, plan on increasing power before the hill has a chance to slow you down.

As you taxi deflect the controls so that the wind cannot easily catch beneath them to produce unstable road handling. For example, a left quartering headwind calls for "up" left aileron along with "up" elevator, while a quartering tailwind from the right asks for "down" elevator and "down" right aileron.

Brake sparingly. Accomplish as much steering as possible with rudder and nosewheel. To avoid riding the brakes, ride with your heels on the floor and the balls of your feet rather than your insteps resting on the rudder pedals (Fig. 1.3). When braking becomes necessary, it's easy to slide your toes up to tap the brakes. Riding the brakes is not only hard on equipment but also causes the fuselage to fishtail. Pilots are usually unaware of this fishtailing; they sit over the wheels at the pivot point. It is the rear-seat passengers who weave nauseatingly from side to side.

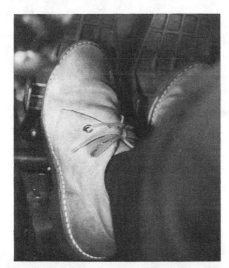

1.3. Prevent dragging the brakes by resting your toes rather than your insteps on the rudder pedals. Keep your heels on the floor.

Prevent a lurching stop when you bring the plane to a stand-still the same way you do in an automobile. Ease off on the brakes and let the plane roll to a stop with light toe pressure in that last moment of travel.

To help ensure smooth taxiing, just imagine a steaming cup of coffee perched above your lap on the instrument panel.

Performing Pretakeoff Checks

Once in the run-up area, position your plane for the pre-takeoff checks. At controlled airports, those with control tow-ers, stop short of the double-striped hold lines (Fig. 1.4). These lines divide the jurisdictions of ground control and the control tower. Point your propwash in a harmless direction and leave room for others to pass by. Park to conserve room on the pad, but not too close to an adjacent plane, particularly if you see that a turned nosewheel will make its first move toward you. (Likewise be sure to come to a stop with *your* nosewheel or tailwheel in the straight-

1.4. Remain short of the double-striped hold lines until takeoff clearance is given.

ahead position.) Be cautious of the direction that propwash or jet blast will take when larger planes turn toward the runway. (Even a corporate-size jet puts out a breakaway puff that is hazardous for 200 feet.)

Just as in starting the engine, a checklist is necessary for a professional pretakeoff check. Here are fifteen items you may wish to include in your list.

1. Brakes: hold or set.
2. Instruments: normal and/or set.
   Clock
   Airspeed indicator
   Attitude indicator
   Altimeter
   Magnetic compass
   Turn indictor
   Heading indicator
   Vertical speed indicator
   Fuel gauges
   Oil-temperature gauge/cylinder temperature
   Oil-pressure gauge
   Ammeter
   Tachometer
3. Controls: free and proper movement.
4. Trim tab: set for takeoff.
5. Seat belts and harnesses: check.
6. Windows and doors: secure.
7. Fuel selector: proper for takeoff.
8. Auxiliary fuel pump: on or as required.
9. Fuel mixture: full rich or as required.
10. Magnetos: check.
11. Carburetor heat: clear for ice and check proper operation.
12. Propeller: cycle and return to high rpm.
13. Flaps: cycle and set for takeoff.
14. Avionics: frequencies, modes, and radials set.
15. Brakes: release.

Each of these checklist items has its own story to tell in the run-up area.

BRAKES: HOLD OR SET. Hold the toe brakes or set the hand brakes before you start working through the checklist. It is so very easy, with all the noise and motion in the run-up area, to allow an unnoticed creep.

INSTRUMENTS: NORMAL AND/OR SET. Each and every gauge on the instrument panel has its own proper readout as you sit in the run-up area. Check the instruments in a logical sequence so that none is overlooked. The system I use reads the gauges from left to right, starting with the top row and working all the way across the panel before dropping to the next row. As I sit in the cockpit of a Piper Cherokee, making notes for this chapter, the instruments come in the sequence that follows.

Clock. Make sure your plane's clock is set and running. It is annoying to discover, well into the flight (with gas gauges dwindling) that the clock and your wristwatch are 45 minutes out of agreement. It is a good idea, with the takeoff near at hand, to make a written note of your departure time.

Airspeed Indicator. The airspeed indicator should read zero with the plane at rest. Take a moment to remind yourself which is the nautical scale and which the statute.

Attitude Indicator. Adjust the attitude indicator's nose dot so that it reads level as you sit in the run-up area. (If you fly a tailwheel, of course, the indication on the ground should read nose high.) Check the suction gauge for sufficient vacuum at this time. The careful pilot has already taken a quick glance for any "banked" display as the plane taxied through turns on its way to the runway. Any bank in excess of 5 degrees during a level taxi turn means that the instrument is worn and unreliable.

Altimeter. Turn the altimeter's Kollsman to the current altimeter setting or, if unavailable, set the instrument to field elevation. Do not be surprised to see a small discrepancy between the indicated altitude and field elevation when adjusting the Kollsman to the altimeter setting. The published field elevation represents the highest point on any usable runway. There is bound to be a discrepancy between that point and the run-up area's elevation. Also, altimeters are calibrated to an average cockpit height of 15 feet when they are manufactured. So don't be concerned by a small discrepancy. If the error exceeds 75 feet, however, consider the instrument unserviceable.

Magnetic Compass. Check the compass against a known heading (squared or paralleled with the runway, for example). See that the instrument's face is filled with fluid and that the compass card rides level.

Turn Indicator. The turn needle should indicate the proper direction of turn, and the ball should move freely *away* from the direction of turns during taxi. When parked in the run-up area, the turn needle should show a zero rate of turn. Turn indicators in most modern light aircraft are electrically driven and operate independently from the vacuum system.

Heading Indicator. Align the heading indicator with the magnetic compass. If you had already set the instrument prior to taxi, you can evaluate its condition prior to takeoff. The heading indicator, if serviceable, should drift no more than 3 degrees per 10 minutes of operation. This instrument's gyroscope requires about a minute of warm-up after starting to attain stability and accuracy.

Vertical Speed Indicator. The vertical speed indicator has a proper readout even before flight. If the needle does not indicate zero, make note of its indication. *That* indication will represent level flight. If, for example, the needle rests on 100 fpm (feet per minute) "up" then that indicates level flight. A climb of 400 fpm would show on the dial as 500 fpm.

Fuel Gauges. Fuel gauges are not precision instruments. They often give a slightly erroneous reading and cannot be depended on to register the exact amount of gas in the tanks. (That can only be verified by visual measure before operating the plane.) Some gauges are even *designed* to register "full" until a specified number of gallons are consumed. You should satisfy yourself, however, that their indications do approximate the known fuel quantity aboard.

Oil-Temperature Gauge. Verify that the engine temperature is in the green arc before you take off. A cold engine may run rough and not deliver full takeoff power. An engine that runs hot in the run-up area, unless you see the cause and can bring the temperature down, may be a signal of engine malfunction. (But don't just *assume* that the temperature will correct itself once under way.)

Oil-Pressure Gauge. The oil-pressure needle should remain within the operating range, even at low rpm. If it does not, either the oil pressure is insufficient to lubricate the engine, or the gauge is defective. Either problem could cause engine damage.

Ammeter. Give the ammeter one final check for normal operation before flight. Should the instrument later show an alternator malfunction in flight that cannot be corrected by resetting, turn off the alternator half of the master switch. Then switch off nonessential accessories to conserve electrical consumption since only battery power will then be available. The engine will not quit; the ignition system receives its power from the magnetos, not the electrical system.

Tachometer. Tachometers do malfunction, and once in flight it is very difficult to set power by reference to engine sound alone. Look for two possible instrument discrepancies as you sit in the run-up area. First, does the needle hold steady? A needle with erratic movement warns of a tachometer about ready to quit. Second, does the instrument indicate an rpm that makes sense with the low power that you are running? If, for example, you are running just slightly more than idle and 2000 or so rpm's are indicated, something is obviously wrong.

You will be sitting in the run-up area for several minutes as you perform your before-takeoff checks. If you leave the engine at idle power for that length of time, the spark plugs are apt to foul. Avoid this fouling, which robs the engine of power, with a setting of 1000 to 1200 rpm.

CONTROLS: FREE AND PROPER MOVEMENT. The control surfaces (ailerons, rudder, and elevators) are manipulated by a system of cables, pulleys, and pushrods — all hidden from visual inspection within the plane's structure. By all means check these controls for full travel and feel for any binding.

Also visually check both ailerons for proper direction of travel. When you turn the yoke to the left, the right aileron deflects downward and the left aileron moves upward. A right turn on the yoke lowers the left aileron, while the right one moves up. If you are flying a model with rear windows in the cockpit, look aft to check the proper movement of elevators and rudder (Fig. 1.5). A

1.5. Some light planes allow rudder and elevator movement to be observed from the cockpit.

word here about those throw-over yokes: if you anticipate the passenger using the controls, rehearse a throw-over while still on the ground. This rehearsal makes sure the system is in working order and that each pilot knows the moves.

TRIM TAB: SET FOR TAKEOFF. An out-of-trim aircraft holds the potential for a deadly takeoff. Cockpit distraction is the usual culprit. Imagine some of the distractions that can come a pilot's way at rotation: a door pops open, the seat slides back, a passenger's feet tangle with the rudder pedals. Then imagine the confused pilot momentarily ignoring the primary responsibility, flying the airplane. If the plane is out-of-trim nose high, a stall is a very real possibility. If trimmed nose low, a dive into the ground is a reasonable prospect. Adverse rudder trim, of course, could easily lead to an inadvertent turn, then a dive. A properly trimmed airplane, on the other hand, gives a distracted pilot a moment to gather thoughts.

Check the trim-control wheel for freedom of movement and exercise the trim to maximum deflections before you set the trim for takeoff. As you set the trim, don't just assume that "neutral" is the proper takeoff setting. Refer to the aircraft manual. Many light aircraft call for different settings, depending on aircraft loading — some as much as 5 degrees from neutral.

SEAT BELTS AND HARNESSES: CHECK. FARs require every adult aboard to occupy a seat and to have belt and harness secured before takeoff. This is for their own safety, and I think it prudent for the pilot to confirm the fact with a good yank on each belt.

But the FARs go further. At the time of this writing, each child below the age of two must be held by an adult. Many think that this regulation flies in the face of reason. Some feel it would be safer if the FAR required the child to be in a restraint seat, as in an automobile. If you carry children, you may want to discuss this with your regional FAA accident prevention specialist before deciding on your own procedure.

WINDOWS AND DOORS: SECURE. Make sure all doors are
closed and locked. If a door should pop open during takeoff,
know there is no cause for alarm. With most light aircraft it will
not adversely affect the airplane, and the slipstream will keep it
fairly tight against the fuselage.

FUEL SELECTOR: PROPER FOR TAKEOFF. It is necessary to set the
fuel-selector handle to the proper position before flight. In
some airplanes all tanks do not feed satisfactorily in a lift-off attitude or steep turn. So if the aircraft's manual recommends a certain tank for takeoff, use it.

AUXILIARY FUEL PUMP: ON. You taxied with the electric auxiliary fuel pump turned off to make certain the engine fuel
pump was functioning. Now, return the boost pump to the "on"
position. As a general rule I use the electric fuel pump any time
that I'm flying within a thousand feet of the ground. I feel that this
practice does not add unwarranted wear to the pump, and it guards
against a potentially dangerous interruption of power should the
engine-driven pump fail at low altitude.

FUEL MIXTURE: FULL RICH OR AS REQUIRED. The fuel mixture
should be run at full rich regardless of altitude any time the
engine is producing over 75 percent of power. This mixture helps
cool the engine and since such high-power operation is usually of
short duration, spark plug fouling from an overrich mixture is
seldom a problem. So at normally anticipated field elevations, use
a full-rich mixture to help cool the engine during the full-power
takeoff.

There may be occasions when the density altitude of your
departure airport exceeds 5000 feet. In these cases, your takeoff
fuel mixture needs leaning in order to prevent a rough-running
engine of impaired power. The typical light-aircraft engine does not
require the cooling effects of a full-rich mixture in the thinner air.
At such altitudes these engines simply will not develop an excess of
75 percent power, even when under full throttle. To lean an engine

at these high-altitude airports, run the engine to full throttle for a moment while you adjust the mixture just as you would in cruise flight.

MAGNETOS: CHECK. When checking the magnetos individually, test the mag position farthest from the "both" position first. This helps to prevent a pilot from inadvertently launching on only one magneto after finishing the checks. It is difficult to visually confirm whether the key has been returned to "both" or the first magneto only (Fig. 1.6). If that first magneto is checked last, however, this error will not easily happen. Each aircraft manual states a recommended rpm for the magneto tests.

1.6. Checking the farthest magneto position first removes the possibility of launching on a single mag.

CARBURETOR HEAT: CLEAR FOR ICE AND CHECK FOR PROPER OPERATION. I like to check the carburetor heat for proper operation *after* I have checked the magnetos. Then, if I have inadvertently left the switch on one mag only, the mistake shows up as an excessive drop in rpm's. The overrich mixture that carburetor heat imposed is just more than one spark plug can successfully fire.

When you apply carburetor heat during the run-up, you are checking for the existence of ice as well as for correct functioning of the heater. Induction icing can easily form during taxiing at low power. A ten-second carburetor heat test quickly reveals any ice by a momentary excessive power drop and rough engine, as melted ice flows through to the engine.

PROPELLER: CYCLE AND RETURN TO FINE PITCH. If you are flying a plane with a controllable prop, test the pitch control before takeoff. Set the power at 1800 rpm or as recommended (adequate to operate pitch) and move the blades to coarse pitch. Satisfactory operation is indicated by a 100–400 rpm loss of power. On very cold days you may need to exercise the control two or three times to obtain a good indication. Return the propeller to fine pitch so the engine can accept full takeoff power once the test is satisfactory.

FLAPS: CYCLE AND SET FOR TAKEOFF. Extend and retract the flaps to their fullest extension to test for operation. Look and feel for any erratic movement or binding, then set for takeoff as recommended by the aircraft's manual.

AVIONICS: FREQUENCIES, MODES, AND RADIALS SET. Adjust all communication and navigation aids for their first anticipated airborne uses. Established procedure for changing from ground control to tower frequency is a bit fuzzy. I prefer to stay on ground frequency until I am finished with my pretakeoff checks. I am, after all, still under the jurisdiction of ground control until I contact the tower for takeoff clearance, and ground may have information to impart during those minutes in the run-up area.

BRAKES: RELEASE. Release the brakes and prepare to take the runway once the pretakeoff checks are complete.

Taking the Runway

Perform the fourth step of your takeoff sequence, taking the runway, with precision. At controlled airports be ready to move onto the runway before you request takeoff clearance. The controller's "cleared for takeoff" implies a need for promptness. Delayed cockpit chores — closing a door, checking passengers' belts, setting a navaid — can easily interrupt the tower's planned traffic flow.

A word here about the tower's "cleared for *immediate* takeoff." That clearance is in reality an *option* given to the pilot, not a demand for instant action. This clearance means that *if* you have the ability to execute an instantaneous departure, you have permission to do so; but if you do *not* have this ability, you have the option to wait until the tower's need for haste is past — to receive a normal takeoff clearance. It is *your* option. Unless highly skilled, you would do best to decline with, "Negative immediate takeoff." For the moderately skilled pilot, the immediate-takeoff maneuver usually follows the antics of a Keystone Kops chase filled with error upon error.

If you are departing an uncontrolled field without the protection of a tower, you must assure traffic clearance for yourself. The only way to do this is to cut a full circle before you take the runway (in addition to a unicom announcement). You cannot be content to just clear the final and base of the runway that you intend to use. *All* runways are legally active at uncontrolled airports — even the *opposite* end of *your* runway. If there are other planes crowding the run-up area, you may need to back-taxi down the taxiway for circling room.

Once cleared and ready to take the runway, quickly pick up the taxiway center line with your nosewheel and follow it to the runway's center stripes. Position your plane directly astride those runway stripes. This precise positioning is desirable for two reasons. First, by beginning your takeoff run from dead center, you conserve runway width that just may be needed if an unexpected swerve (blown tire?) occurs. Second, runways are laid with a crown for drainage. Taking off on the sloping side surface invites loss of directional control.

Once astride the center stripes, with the nosewheel aimed straight ahead, you are ready to begin the next segment of your takeoff sequence.

Making the Takeoff Run

The takeoff run asks the pilot for three precise actions:

1. The most rapid acceleration possible to rotate speed.
2. Positive directional control.
3. Correction for any crosswind.

ACCELERATION. A smooth hand on the throttle is the first step toward rapid acceleration on the takeoff run. A throttle advanced too quickly is very likely to feed fuel to the engine faster than the cylinders can digest it. Then, the engine will falter and significantly reduce acceleration. The best power application has the pilot smoothly advancing the throttle as fast as the engine can take it without giving any audible signal or misfire. Once full throttle is applied, glance quickly at the tachometer. Is the engine performing 100 percent, or does anemic power indication suggest an abort?

Deflected control surfaces add considerable drag as speed increases on the takeoff run, reducing acceleration. Allow the control surfaces to streamline unless there is a reason to move them, such as needing to correct for a crosswind. Some pilots develop the habit of "walking" the rudder for directional control during the takeoff run. Not only is this an ineffective way to keep the plane going straight, but each wiggle of that rudder fin adds drag to slow the action (Fig. 1.7). Other pilots attempt to use differential braking to keep the plane going straight. This not only invites a swerve but also drastically retards acceleration.

Some pilots feel they can assist acceleration by lifting the nosewheel as soon as ground speed permits. Their thinking is to reduce the rolling friction of the wheel against the runway. When we lift that nosewheel, we increase the wing's angle of attack and create lift, which in turn creates aerodynamic drag. Acceleration is im-

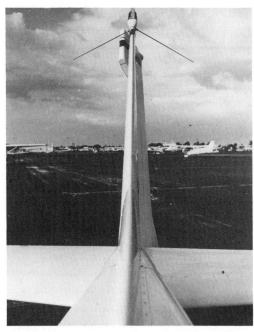

1.7. A deflected rudder increases drag.

paired if this occurs too early in the takeoff run. Conversely, however, do not press the control wheel forward. This throws pressure against that nosewheel and creates undue rolling friction. It is best to let the control surfaces streamline unless there is a real need for control deflection that takes precedence over acceleration.

DIRECTIONAL CONTROL. Rudder and steerable nosewheel are the principal tools of directional control during the takeoff run. The best way to keep the brakes out of this steering action is to keep your heels on the floor. Doing so keeps your toes from inadvertently pressing the brakes, yet you can quickly slide your foot up should you need to stop the plane.

The aerodynamic force of *slipstream effect* tries to disturb your directional control during the takeoff run—it tries to slew your plane to the left. Slipstream effect is caused by propwash. The downward-swinging blade in the right-hand half of the propeller arc pushes the air under the fuselage. This slipstream then corkscrews up around the left side of the plane and flows upward to strike the left side of the vertical stabilizer (Fig. 1.8). This, of course, tends to slew the plane to the left. Slipstream effect is most apparent during the first few moments of the takeoff run, right

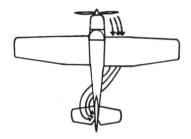

1.8. Slipstream effect causes the plane to veer left.

after full throttle is applied. It takes quick right rudder to keep the plane astride the center line.

Some pilots experience difficulty with directional control simply because they are unaware of the effect that *aileron drag* has on the takeoff run. Aileron drag (also called *adverse yaw*) occurs when you turn the control wheel. It means that when you turn the control wheel in one direction, the *airplane* turns in the opposite direction. If you turn the wheel to the right, for instance, the right aileron is elevated and shielded from the onrushing wind by the wing's curved upper surface (Fig. 1.9). The left aileron, on the other hand, dips beneath the wing's flat lower surface, digs into the wind, and the airplane slews left.

1.9. With the crosswind blowing from the right, the pilot has lowered the left aileron into the slipstream. The right aileron is protected from the slipstream by the wing's curved upper surface.

A problem arises when some pilots try to correct a slew by instinctively turning the control wheel *away* from the slew—a reversion to a car's steering wheel, I believe. But this action only further intensifies the slew with aileron drag. As an example, picture a plane drifting off center line to the right. The pilot erroneously tries to correct by turning the wheel to the left. This move lowers the right aileron into the wind and the plane drifts even farther to the right of center line. The proper action, naturally, would have been to correct with the rudder and nosewheel steering.

CROSSWIND CORRECTION. A crosswind needs correcting during the takeoff run, just as it does in the landing roll. In either case the wind blows against that vertical stabilizer to weather-vane the plane into the wind.

Your primary defense here is the positive use of aileron drag. By turning the control wheel to deflect the downwind aileron downward, you produce drag against the direction of the crosswind. Let's say that the crosswind is from the left. Turn the control wheel in that direction and the right aileron digs down into the onrushing air. Now, the crosswind tries to swing the plane left, but aileron drag counters with its right-hand pull to keep the plane on center line (Fig. 1.10).

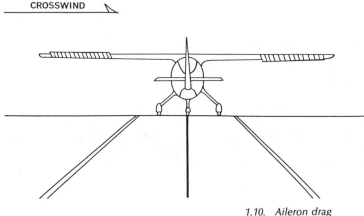

CROSSWIND

1.10. Aileron drag counters with its pull against the left crosswind to keep the plane on center line.

The question is how much aileron to use. Well, it is practically impossible to use too much aileron as the takeoff roll begins. The initial ground speed is so slow that the down aileron produces only minimal drag. So, begin the roll with full control deflection. Two things happen as ground speed increases. First, drag increases with speed — double the speed, for example, and drag quadruples. Second, the crosswind does not affect a faster-moving plane as much as a slower-moving one. (It's a condition of time and force.) So, as the plane accelerates down the runway, start decreasing aileron. Time this decrease of control deflection so that the full deflection is steadily reduced to near-zero aileron deflection just as you lift off.

Each make and model of airplane has a maximum crosswind component that it can safely accept. There is a limit beyond which there is just not enough aileron drag to do the job. This crosswind component is often stated in the plane's manual, but if not, apply a rule of thumb: do not attempt a takeoff when the crosswind component exceeds one-third of the plane's stall speed. To estimate the crosswind component, use these guidelines.

1. If the wind lies within 30 degrees of runway alignment, estimate the crosswind component at one-half the wind's velocity.
2. If the wind lies from 30 to 60 degrees across the runway, estimate the crosswind component at three-fourths the wind's velocity.
3. If the wind lies from 60 to 90 degrees across the runway, estimate the component to equal the velocity (Fig. 1.11).

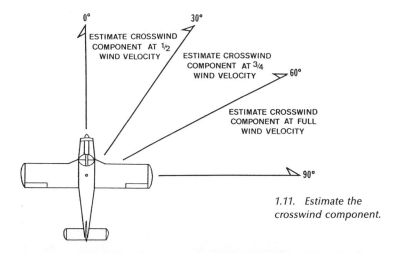

1.11. Estimate the crosswind component.

If ground control's statement of wind is not available, look to the wind sock for both wind angle to the runway and velocity. The sock is designed to stiffen at 15 knots. A sock drooping at a 45-degree angle, for example, shows a velocity of 7 or 8 knots (Fig. 1.12).

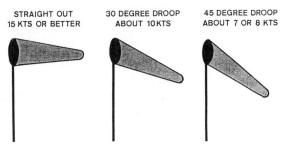

STRAIGHT OUT
15 KTS OR BETTER

30 DEGREE DROOP
ABOUT 10 KTS

45 DEGREE DROOP
ABOUT 7 OR 8 KTS

1.12. A wind sock is designed to stiffen at 15 knots. Estimate lesser velocities by the sock's angle of droop.

As you roll down the runway, keep in mind the three primary pilot responsibilities during the takeoff run: rapid acceleration, directional control, crosswind correction. Do a good job with these and you are in good shape to perform the next step of your takeoff sequence, lifting off.

Lifting Off

The lift-off stage of the takeoff asks the pilot to perform two primary duties during the segment's short duration:

1. Precisely control airspeed.
2. Accurately control direction by effectively correcting for crosswind and compensating for P factor.

AIRSPEED CONTROL. If you try to lift off before the wings are ready to fly, you lengthen the takeoff distance. Aerodynamic drag of the wing's angle of attack is the culprit. Try to hold the plane groundbound beyond the wing's desire to fly and again take-off distance is lengthened. In this case, it is the rolling friction of the tires that slows the action.

The lift-off stage of the takeoff begins with your first back pressure on the yoke. Study the manual for the aircraft you are flying to determine just when this should occur. (And let me say here that you *should* possess a copy of the aircraft's manual. All too often this is not the case with renter pilots. It is very chancy to just assume that the plane under you at the moment will behave just like another model with which you are more familiar.) Most aircraft manuals are quite specific on the subject of lift-off — rotation speed, lift-off speed, pitch control, and the like. Follow the manufacturer's recommendations to the letter. That manufacturer has determined the very best procedures to follow.

DIRECTIONAL CONTROL. There are two forces that try to impair directional control at lift-off; crosswind and P factor. You have reduced aileron deflection to near zero at the moment of lift-off. Yet the crosswind still exists and must remain corrected if you are to climb out astride the center line. So, as the wheels clear the runway, make a coordinated turn into the wind to establish a wind-correction angle. Once this angle is pinned down, just roll the wings level and proceed with the climbout. The wind-correction crab angle that holds a steady course near the ground will likely hold the course throughout your initial climbout. True, the plane's speed increases during this time, but the crosswind's velocity also increases with each yard of altitude.

Knowing, at the outset, the approximate wind-correction angle that will do the job is helpful. Use a rule of thumb: at the usual light-plane lift-off speeds of 55 to 65 knots, correct 1 degree for each knot of crosswind component. Thus, a 10-degree wind-correction should keep you on track when lifting off into a 10-knot crosswind.

P factor plays an important role in directional control during lift-off. P factor comes from the propeller's motion. When the plane is pitched upward for lift-off the propeller blade in the right half of the propeller arc has a high angle of attack and develops more pull than the left half of the propeller arc (Fig. 1.13). The plane tends to swing left. Quick right rudder, however, keeps the plane dead on center line.

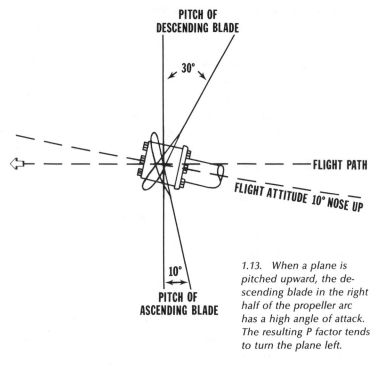

1.13. When a plane is pitched upward, the descending blade in the right half of the propeller arc has a high angle of attack. The resulting P factor tends to turn the plane left.

With the airspeed increasing toward best rate and with directional control well in hand, you are ready for the next stage of the takeoff sequence, the intial climbout.

Flying the Initial Climbout

The initial climbout segment of your takeoff sequence includes those seconds from lift-off to that height 400 feet or so aloft. There are elements of precision flying that you must deliver if you are to keep the perfection of your takeoff intact during those moments.

First, bear down on airspeed control. Your plane will continue to accelerate from lift-off. If you are holding back pressure that produces best rate of climb speed, the plane will settle to this speed about 50 feet or so above the ground. Once the airspeed indicator hits best rate speed, make any needed readjustment to the trim to hold that speed. Then, if the takeoff employed flaps, start retracting them, one increment at a time, retrimming to hold the speed with each retraction. This slow flap retraction prevents "dumping" flaps. Pilots who dump all the flaps immediately after takeoff find that airspeed control is nearly impossible to maintain. They may also suffer an actual loss of altitude on the initial climbout and bring their plane dangerously close to its flaps-up stall speed.

Once best rate of climb speed is well established, raise the gear if you are flying a retractable. Watch the airspeed indicator as you do and move the nose to keep the airspeed captured. Then retrim. It's a good idea to delay retracting the gear until this time. Pilots who immediately retract at lift-off and find the need to get back onto the ground could forget to lower the gear again in the excitement.

Directional control is vital during the intial climbout. Again, crosswind and the left-turning tendency of torque try to move you off course. But stay astride the runway center line. When you see the runway disappearing beneath you, pick out two landmarks straight ahead to help keep runway alignment. If you let your plane drift, you might find that the first turn from the pattern places you directly in front of a faster plane taking off behind you (Fig. 1.14).

Expend considerable effort toward traffic avoidance during the initial climbout. Let your efforts follow two lines:

1. Spotting other planes.
2. Making yourself more visible to other pilots.

When you look for other planes, search that band of sky 3 inches above and below the horizon and scan each sector of sky. After

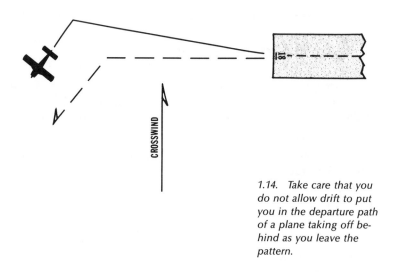

1.14. Take care that you do not allow drift to put you in the departure path of a plane taking off behind as you leave the pattern.

turning your head toward each sector, move your *eyes* rather than your head for an unblurred look. And remember that your eyes work like a telescope; you must vary your range of focus. We tend to focus only out to the horizon—and look right through a nearby plane.

Once away from the runway, do everything possible to protect yourself from *unseen* traffic; alert them to you. Keep your landing light blazing while in the traffic area. You may not see the head-on traffic (the toughest of all to spot), but they should certainly see you. By the same token, turn on your strobes if you have them. They are quite visible even during daylight. (A red rotating beacon, on the other hand, is of little value during the bright day. You usually see the plane before you see the beacon.) Depart with your transponder on. A controller will see your blip and warn participating traffic of your presence even if you are not in touch with Air Traffic Control (ATC).

Fly your initial climbout with precise airspeed control, directional control, and traffic avoidance in mind. Then, at pattern altitude, initiate the next stage of your takeoff sequence, the pattern departure.

Leaving the Pattern

Continue the takeoff's follow-through with a precision pattern departure. There are two prescribed standard pattern exits: if departing the traffic pattern, either continue straight out, or exit with a 45-degree turn (left or right according to the airport's pattern flow) beyond the departure end of the runway and after reaching pattern altitude. (Old pelicans will find that the previous initial 90-degree turn, followed by a 45-degree exit is obsolete. That often puts you into conflict with arriving traffic in today's congested traffic pattern.)

At a controlled airport, of course, the tower is usually quite willing to sanction a pilot request for a nonstandard departure that more quickly puts you on course. Just remember that you need to make the request and receive a clearance before straying from established procedure.

Climbing to Cruise Altitude

Continue your alertness for traffic as you climb toward cruise altitude. Many aircraft hide much of the forward visibility with the cowl when in the climb attitude. The pilot is wise to clear for head-on traffic every several seconds during this time. Either make a shallow S-turn of 20 degrees either side of the flight path or slightly lower the nose for a quick look-see ahead.

Use the climb-power setting and airspeed recommended by the plane's flight manual. Some pilots feel that they save the engine by either reducing power or climbing at a shallow angle with a higher airspeed. Either move is a mistake. That plane's manufacturer knows what is best for its airplane. You may find, when flying behind a controllable-pitch prop, that the manifold pressure drops below the recommended number as you continue to climb toward thinner and thinner air. The solution is to monitor the engine gauges and increase throttle each thousand feet as needed to keep manifold pressure right on the mark.

When departing through an area of heavy arrivals and departures, it is best not to drastically alter your pattern-exit heading until you pass through 2500 AGL (above ground level) or reach the 5-mile airport traffic area limit. To do otherwise may put you on a conflicting course with arrivals or heavier aircraft flying a wide 2000-foot-high pattern.

Once well clear of the traffic area, pick up a heading that gives you a 30-degree intercept angle with the airway or course you intend to travel. This 30-degree intercept heading is sharp enough to move you on course in a reasonable time and provides an easy "turn-on" when you reach the airway.

Leveling to Cruise

Fly the final follow-through stage, leveling to cruise, as a precision maneuver. Plan your level-off so that cruise speed is attained just as you lower the nose to cruise attitude, at the exact desired altitude, and with the ball in the cage throughout. That's a tough bill to fill. With practice and concentration, you will hit the mark every time. To make the maneuver easier, think of your level-off procedure as a sequence of four steps.

STEP 1. Start lowering the nose 50 feet below your intended cruise altitude for each 500 fpm on the vertical speed indicator (VSI). A 400 fpm rate of climb, for example, calls for a 40-foot lead; 600 fpm asks a 60-foot lead. Time a smooth reduction in pitch so that the nose levels just as you reach cruise altitude. It is helpful to monitor the upward-creeping altimeter as you watch the nose settle toward the level attitude. It is just a matter of making your milk and cookies finish together.

STEP 2. With climb power and the nose level, the plane quickly accelerates to cruise speed. Promptly pull the throttle to cruise power the moment the airspeed indicator says "cruising speed." If you reduce the power before this moment you will probably lose 10 or 15 feet; after this moment and you will fly above your cruise altitude.

STEP 3. During the climb you held right rudder against torque to keep the ball in the cage. Continue to keep that ball caged throughout the level-off. Do so by coordinating a steady release of right rudder with the lowering nose as your plane accelerates to cruise speed.

STEP 4. Finally, with cruise speed and power established, make a final trim adjustment, fine-tune the power setting, and lean the mixture to its cruise fuel flow.

Ten separate stages of the takeoff sequence have brought us from the ramp area to our cruise altitude. Separate steps allowed us to bring our concentration into focus, perform the maneuver itself, and provide a follow-through. Carry this reasoning to the cockpit and you will make perfect takeoff after perfect takeoff.

IN REVIEW: Normal Takeoffs

PREFLIGHT REMINDERS

- To think of a departure as only those moments of takeoff run and lift-off practically guarantees a takeoff lacking in concentration and accuracy.
- Perform your takeoff as a sequence of ten steps that provide an address, a delivery, and a follow-through.

1. Starting the engine
   - Prime considerations when starting the engine must include the safety of those in and around the airplane and the protection of the power plane and airframe accessories.
   - Abide by a written checklist to achieve a professional and precise engine start.
   - FARs require the pilot to instruct passengers in the fastening and unfastening of their harness and seat belt.

- Improper seat position is often the reason for erratic rudder control.
- Squat switches do not guarantee that an "up" gear switch will not retract the wheels while still on the ground.
- Consult your aircraft manual to determine the proper take-off tank.
- Hot air from an open carburetor heat produces an overrich mixture during taxi, which promotes plug fouling.
- Do not attempt to start an engine by hand propping unless you have had instruction in the procedure.
- Consult the airplane's manual to determine the proper use of mixture control during engine start.
- Avoid starting the engine with excess throttle.
- After yelling, Clear! take a moment to visually clear for pedestrians before starting.
- Hold or set the brakes to prevent the plane from jumping ahead at engine start.
- If the engine is difficult to start, avoid prolonged cranking that may damage the starter armature.
- If the recommended starting procedure does not readily fire the engine, the engine may require attention.
- The majority of engine wear occurs during its first moments of operation, requiring a low-power warm-up.

2. Taxiing to the runway
   - When taxiing, remember that other pilots are probably not looking.
   - Once under way, plan ahead in order to maintain a constant taxi speed.
   - Brake sparingly; accomplish as much steering as possible with rudder and nosewheel.
   - Deflect control surfaces so the wind cannot catch beneath them.

3. Performing pretakeoff checks
   - Adhere to a written checklist to accomplish a professional and complete pretakeoff check.

- An attitude indicator that registers a "bank" in excess of 5 degrees during a taxiing turn is worn and unreliable.
- The altimeter may be unserviceable if its error exceeds 75 feet.
- The heading indicator, if serviceable, should drift no more than 3 degrees per 10 minutes of operation.
- An out-of-trim aircraft holds the potential for a disastrous takeoff.
- Testing the magneto farthest from the "both" position first helps to prevent inadvertently taking off on a single mag.
- Consult the plane's manual to determine the flap setting that is correct for takeoff.

4. Taking the runway
   - Unless highly skilled, avoid opting for the tower's immediate-takeoff option.
   - Clear for traffic at an uncontrolled field with a full-circle taxiing turn.
   - Position your plane directly astride the runway's center stripes.

5. Making the takeoff run
   - The takeoff run asks for rapid acceleration and positive directional control, including crosswind and P-factor corrections.
   - Rapid acceleration calls for a smooth throttle, streamlined control surfaces, and minimal rolling friction.
   - Rudder and the steerable nosewheel are the principal tools of directional control; avoid differential braking.
   - It is practically impossible to use too much aileron for crosswind correction during the initial seconds of the takeoff run.
   - The left-turning tendency of slipstream effect is most pronounced during the initial moments of the takeoff run.
   - Aileron drag during the takeoff run causes reverse steering by the ailerons.

- Each make and model has a maximum crosswind component that it can accept.

6. Lifting off
   - Either a too-soon or a too-late rotation will lengthen the takeoff distance.
   - Follow the manufacturer's recommended rotate speed to the letter.
   - P factor at lift-off tends to slew your plane to the left.

7. Flying the initial climbout
   - Trim is important to airspeed control during the climb; reset it for both gear and each increment of flap retractions.
   - Begin looking for arriving traffic the moment you are safely away.

8. Leaving the pattern
   - There are two standard pattern exits: straight out, or with a 45-degree turn at pattern altitude.

9. Climbing to cruise altitude
   - Shallow S-turns of 20 degrees help spot traffic hidden by the nose cowl.
   - Closely adhere to the manufacturer's recommended best rate of climb speed and power setting.

10. Leveling to cruise
    - Start lowering the nose 50 feet below the intended altitude for each 500 fpm on the VSI.
    - With the plane level, delay reducing power until you reach cruise speed.

- During level-off, keep the ball centered by anticipating the effect that increasing speed and diminishing power have on torque.

IN-FLIGHT AIDS

ENGINE-STARTING CHECKLIST

1. Seat belt and harness: fastened
2. Seat position: locked in track
3. Landing gear: down and locked
4. Fuel selector: freedom of movement; proper tank
5. Cowl flaps: open
6. Carburetor heat: cold
7. Propeller: set for high rpm
8. Avionics and electrical equipment: off
9. Fuel mixture: full rich or as required
10. Throttle: start position
11. Primer pump: prime cylinders
12. Propeller area clear!
13. Electrical master switch: on
14. Auxiliary fuel pump: on
15. Brakes: hold or set
16. Magnetos: on
17. Start engine: avoid prolonged cranking
18. Throttle: set for warm-up (1000–1200 rpm)
19. Oil pressure: normal within 30 seconds
20. Ammeter: normal
21. Brakes: clear area and release
22. Other items: _____
    _____
    _____

1.15. Items to include in the engine-starting checklist. Consult the aircraft manual for variations or additional items.

PRETAKEOFF CHECKLIST

1. Brakes: set or hold
2. Instruments: normal and/or set
   Magnetic compass: check fluid level; verify indication
   Clock: note time off
   Airspeed indicator: zero reading
   Attitude indicator: set for level flight
   Altimeter: Kollsman set; 75-foot maximum error
   Turn indicator: checked during taxi
   Heading indicator: set
   Vertical speed indicator: note any error
   Fuel gauge: one-fourth-tank minimum for takeoff
   Oil/cylinder temperature: normal
   Oil-pressure gauge: normal
   Ammeter: normal
   Tachometer: needle steady
3. Controls: free and proper movement
4. Trim tab: cycle and set for takeoff
5. Seat belts and harness: check passengers
6. Doors and windows: secure
7. Fuel selector: takeoff tank
8. Magnetos: _____rpm drop; _____rpm differential
9. Carburetor heat: check for ice; check operation (_____rpm)
10. Propeller: cycle and return to fine pitch (_____rpm)
11. Mixture: verify full rich or as required
12. Flaps: cycle and set for takeoff
13. Avionics: frequencies, modes, radials, set
14. Brakes: clear area and release
15. Other items: _____
    _____
    _____

1.16. Items to include in pretakeoff checklist. Consult aircraft manual for variations or additional items.

CLIMB CHECKLIST

1. Engine temperature: monitor for normal
2. Oil pressure: monitor for normal
3. Power: advance throttle as needed to maintain climb power
   (_____rpm; _____mp)
4. Mixture: lean as required; best power _____ degrees below EGT peak
5. Other:_____

1.17. Items to include in climb checklist. Consult aircraft manual for variations or additional items.

CRUISE CHECKLIST

1. Cowl flaps: close
2. Power: set for cruise altitudes:
   55%_____rpm / _____mp
   65%_____rpm / _____mp
   75%_____rpm / _____mp
3. Mixture: lean to altitude; cruise lean _____degrees
4. Trim: set for level flight
5. Engine gauges: monitor throughout flight
6. Fuel selector: switch tanks each hour; avoid running a tank dry
7. Fuel gauges: calculate time remaining each hour; plan landing with one-quarter capacity and/or one hour remaining
8. Others: _____
   _____
   _____

1.18. Items to include in cruise checklist. Consult aircraft manual for variations or additional items. (For checklists to use before landing, after clearing runway, and during shut down, refer to Fowler, Making Perfect Landings in Light Airplanes, Iowa State University Press, 1984.)

I again become aware that no pilot alive can resist watching a plane take off. He may pass a motionless airplane without noticing it, but the moment his ears detect the first burst of power from a plane, however distant, he will turn his head regardless of everything else around him and watch it.

—**Ernest K. Gann**
Fate Is the Hunter

CHAPTER TWO

Short-Field Takeoffs

The drowsy summer day was well under way. Cicadas sang, and the aroma of pine wafted across the infield to mix with the perfume of a freshly mown runway. The arrival's third go-around brought the rural airport hang-arounders to their feet. They left their makeshift chairs of red Craftsman tool chests and cased Aeroshell and moved as a group from the weathered wooden hangar out into the warm afternoon sunshine. All noses pointed upward and outward along the strip's departure path. Two hundred horsepower of echoes still bounced through the pine- and beech-covered knolls surrounding the small Smokey Mountain airport.

The clique of onlookers caught sight of the streamlined plane banking to downwind for another go. On this one, the pilot cinched his pattern in tight and killed power with a fierce determination that the folks on the ground felt. The gang scurried over to the vantage point by the sock to enjoy the only excitement that the sleepy airport ever provided, watching a long-runway pilot trying to squeeze a citified airplane into a short-strip mountain airport.

The sleek retractable sank through base like a wounded U-boat, did a little Stuka dive down short final, and landed with a *whump* that would do any carrier pilot proud. Heavy feet on the brakes sent divots flying from the turf as the bounding plane whisked past the wind sock and swung to a lurching stop alongside the line shack.

Personally, I thought the passenger looked a bit tight around the mouth as he stumbled from the cockpit. But the pilot was a picture of confidence as he bent down to count the wheels, ordered the tanks topped, and went in search of a taxicab.

Rented plane, I thought to myself.

I had a flight on and could not stick around to watch the pilot try to track down Bernie, the town's only cabbie. I next saw the pilot two afternoons later. He had returned for departure, passenger in tow (but not following too closely, I noticed). The pilot stuffed the suitcases into the aft hatch and climbed aboard with the passenger. As the pilot fiddled with starting the fuel-injected engine, I saw Gerry, the airport owner, standing nearby, watching. Gerry is a romantic sort; he likes to withhold his help until the last dramatic moment. He didn't make his move until the prop started. Then he moved alongside the churning engine and chopped his hands for the pilot to kill the mags.

"Don't you know you can get into a place you can't get out of?"

Gerry and the pilot then reviewed the plane's performance charts. On landing, the plane needed 1980 feet—a snug fit for the 2800-foot strip, but the pilot had made it. The *takeoff* chart said something worse: with the breezeless midday sun and topped-off tanks, 2580 feet. Too close for safe comfort. If the pilot waited until tomorrow, Gerry explained, the cool morning breeze and defueling to half tanks just might make a takeoff work—and there was a big municipal airport with plenty of gas only 20 minutes down the valley. Gerry was about to suggest they remain overnight when he noticed the passenger already mounting a search for Bernie.

Short-field departures account for more than their fair share of aircraft accidents. Most of these accidents, injuries, and deaths would never have occurred if the pilot had taken two simple steps before the engine ever cranked:

1. Made a pretakeoff study of the plane's takeoff performance tables and carefully related those facts and figures to the takeoff environment at hand.
2. Put into play two simple fail-safe measures that practically guaranteed against tragedy.

Takeoff Variables

Let's discuss that first action, studying the charts and relating them to the takeoff at hand. In order to understand the relationship of the charts' facts and figures to our takeoffs, we need to understand the variables of takeoff performance, which follow.

1. Runway surface conditions.
2. Ground run versus total to clear obstacle.
3. Flaps and airspeed.
4. Field elevation.
5. Runway temperature.
6. Headwind component.
7. Aircraft loading.
8. Pilot technique.

RUNWAY SURFACE CONDITIONS. Many takeoff performance charts contemplate only a dry, paved runway surface (Fig. 2.1). But more often than not, short fields do not offer this ideal runway condition. Many are grass strips, and some of those need mowing. Some have poor drainage and give us the added complication of a wet surface.

In the absence of performance figures concerning a grass surface, apply some rules of thumb.

1. If the grass is well mowed and dry, add 20 percent to the paved-runway "obstacle-clearance distance."
2. If that grass runway needs mowing, or the grass is wet, make that fudge factor 30 percent.
3. If there is actually standing water on an unpaved strip, treat the

4-6

Sierra 200 B24R

NORMAL TAKE-OFF DIST/

ASSOCIATED CONDITIONS:

POWER	2700 RPM, FULL THROTTLE
MIXTURE	LEAN TO FIELD ELEVATION
FLAPS	15°
GEAR	RETRACTED, AFTER LIFT-OFF
RUNWAY	PAVED, LEVEL, DRY SURFACE
WEIGHT	2750 LBS
TAKE-OFF SPEEDS	LIFT-OFF 71 MPH/62 KTS IAS
	50 FT 75 MPH/65 KTS IAS

WIND COMPONENT DOWN RUNWAY KNOTS	SEA LEVEL			2000 FT			
	OAT °F °C	GROUND ROLL FEET	TOTAL OVER 50 FT OBSTACLE FEET	OAT °F °C	GROUND ROLL FEET	TOTAL OVER 50 FT OBSTACLE FEET	OA °F
0	20 -7	1003	1544	20 -7	1172	1837	20
	40 4	1087	1674	40 4	1269	1996	40
	60 16	1174	1812	60 16	1370	2166	60
	80 27	1265	1957	80 27	1474	2346	80
	100 38	1359	2108	100 38	1590	2559	100
15	20 -7	781	1258	20 -7	922	1510	20
	40 4	851	1370	40 4	1003	1648	40
	60 16	924	1489	60 16	1088	1797	60
	80 27	1001	1615	80 27	1176	1955	80
	100 38	1080	1747	100 38	1267	2127	100

2.1. Many takeoff charts contemplate only a paved, dry surface. (Beech Aircraft Corporation; for illustration purposes only, not to be used for flight planning or aircraft operation)

takeoff with a soft-field technique; the distance needed can increase by 50 percent or more.

There is another subject that goes hand in hand with runway surface versus takeoff distance—tire inflation. Underinflated tires can easily increase takeoff distance 10 percent or more. So, if your cross-country flight contemplates a short-field departure, verify tire pressure before you even set out. Consult your plane's operations manual for the exact air pressure needed. The same tire, mounted on different light airplanes, will carry different inflations ranging from 20 psi to 40 psi for proper takeoff performance.

GROUND RUN VERSUS TOTAL TO CLEAR OBSTACLE. Takeoff charts state two distance values for each runway environment: *ground run* and *total distance to clear a 50-foot obstacle* (Fig. 2.2). This total-distance figure, of course, is the sum of the ground run plus the air distance required after the wheels leave the ground (Fig. 2.3). It is this longer total-distance figure that is important to the pilot. This is true whether or not obstacles are present. After all, even without an obstacle, any pilot wants to be at least *that* high as the plane crosses the runway's end.

			AT SEA LEVEL & 59° F.		**AT 2500**
S FT. H	WIND KNOTS	GROUND RUN	TOTAL TO CLEAR 50 FT. OBS		GROUND RUN
)	0	735	1385		910
	10	500	1035		630
	20	305	730		395

Increase the distances 10% for each 35°F. increase For operation on a dry, grass runway, increase dis "total to clear 50 ft. obstacle" figure.

2.2. The total distance to clear an obstacle is the value of most interest to the pilot. (Cessna Aircraft Company; for illustration purposes only, not to be used for flight planning or aircraft operation)

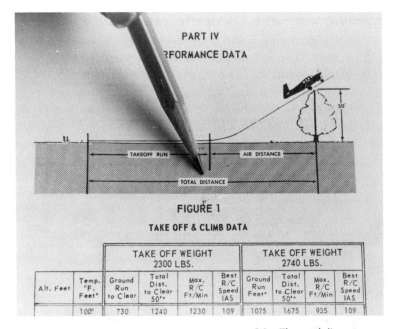

FIGURE 1

TAKE OFF & CLIMB DATA

		TAKE OFF WEIGHT 2300 LBS.				TAKE OFF WEIGHT 2740 LBS.			
Alt. Feet	Temp. °F. Feet*	Ground Run to Clear	Total Dist. to Clear 50'*	Max. R/C Ft/Min	Best R/C Speed IAS	Ground Run Feet*	Total Dist. to Clear 50'*	Max. R/C Ft/Min	Best R/C Speed IAS
	100°	730	1240	1230	109	1075	1675	935	109

2.3. The total-distance value includes ground run and the air-travel distance to gain 50 feet. (Mooney Aircraft, Inc.; for illustration purposes only, not to be used for flight planning or aircraft operation)

When you relate this chart distance to the actual situation at hand, remember one thing. Obstacles do not always come in standard Federal Aviation Administration (FAA) 50-foot heights. Our long-leaf pines here in Florida, for instance, run about 100 feet, and while a single-story building is usually only 15 or 20 feet, you need to add another 10 feet or so for each extra story.

To relate any "nonstandard" high obstacle to your chart

1. Estimate the true height of the obstacle.
2. Subtract the *ground run* distance from the *total distance to clear obstacle* value.

3. Add this distance (air distance) for each 50 feet of estimated obstacle height in excess of the standard 50 feet.

An Example. The takeoff chart now before me shows a *total-distance-to-clear-obstacle* value of 1660 feet for a particular takeoff situation. Of this, 910 feet is *ground run*. By subtracting the little number from the big number, I calculate the *air distance* required for each 50 feet of obstacle height at 750 feet. If I estimate the actual obstacle's height at 100 feet, I add this 750 feet to 1660 for a required total distance of 2410 feet.

FLAPS AND AIRSPEED. Most aircraft manuals are quite specific concerning takeoff flap position (Fig. 2.4). They often recommend two settings, one for normal takeoffs and another for short-field departures over obstacles. The manufacturer has spent untold hours of practical demonstration in order to determine what works best for a maximum performance takeoff. Adhere to that manufacturer's recommendation.

TAKE-OFF DAT

TAKE-OFF DISTANCE WITH 20° FLAPS FROM HA

SS ;HT 5.	IAS @ 50' MPH	HEAD WIND KNOTS	AT SEA LEVEL & 59°F.		AT 2500 FT. & 50°F.		A
			GROUND RUN	TOTAL TO CLEAR 50' OBS	GROUND RUN	TOTAL TO CLEAR 50' OBS	GR
i0	63	0	705	1350	845	1625	
		10	490	1025	595	1245	
		20	310	740	385	910	
i0	58	0	485	955	575	1120	
		10	325	710	395	840	
		20	195	490	245	590	
i0	52	0	295	655	350	745	
		10	185	460	225	530	
		20	105	305	130	355	

2.4. The recommended flap position is normally stated alongside the takeoff chart. (Cessna Aircraft Company; for illustration purposes only, not to be used for flight planning or aircraft operation)

If flaps are called for, it is usually best to leave them extended until you are well beyond any obstacles. An early retraction can cause a momentary loss of climb and bring you dangerously close to a stall when you are climbing at best angle of climb speed.

The aircraft manual will specify three speeds in connection with short-field takeoffs:

1. Rotate (lift-off) speed.
2. Best angle of climb speed.
3. Best rate of climb speed.

Rotate Speed. During the takeoff run you are holding slight back pressure on the stick. Rotate speed is that point at which you apply additional back pressure to gain lift-off. Don't guess at this critical speed when facing a short-field departure. If you use an incorrect lift-off speed, either above or below the stated rotate speed, you will lengthen your takeoff distance. (Remember, if you leave it on the ground too long, you suffer frictional drag; if you try to break away too soon, you suffer aerodynamic drag.) As in the case of flaps, the manufacturer has gone to some lengths to determine just what speed works best for its airplane. Many aircraft manuals state this speed alongside the takeoff performance chart (Fig. 2.5). Others include the speed in the normal-operations section.

Best Angle of Climb Speed. Best angle of climb speed is that precise airspeed that delivers the most altitude for the amount of *horizontal distance* flown. Obviously, it is the speed we want to hit when obstacles reach into our departure path. Again, through trial and error, the manufacturer has determined the speed that best does the job. Any other speed costs you takeoff distance to clear the obstacle. Invariably, this best-angle airspeed is noted in the takeoff chart, often indicated as "IAS at 50 feet" (Fig. 2.6).

I'd like to give a word of caution concerning best angle of climb speed. In most of the lower-powered planes there is no problem — best-angle speed exceeds the power-off stall speed by a safe

TAKE-OFF.

NORMAL TAKE-OFF.

(1) Wing Flaps -- Up.
(2) Carburetor Heat -- Cold.
(3) Power -- Full throttle and 2600 RPM.
(4) Elevator Control -- Raise nosewheel at 60 M
(5) Climb Speed -- 90 MPH until all obstacles a
up climb speed as shown in "NORMAL CLIMB" (

MAXIMUM PERFORMANCE TAKE-OFF.

(1) Wing Flaps -- 20°.

2.5. Rotate speed may be included in the "procedures" section of the manual. (Cessna Aircraft Company; for illustration purposes only, not to be used for flight planning or aircraft operation)

—TAKE-OFF DISTANCE—

ROSS WT. LBS.	IAS 50 FT. MPH	HEAD WIND KNOTS	AT SEA LEVEL & 59° F.		AT 2500 FT. & 50°	
			GROUND RUN	TOTAL TO CLEAR 50 FT. OBS	GROUND RUN	TOTA TO CLE 50 FT. (
1600	70	0	735	1385	910	166(
		10	500	1035	630	125(
		20	305	730	395	89(

OTES: 1. Increase the distances 10% for each 35°F. increase in tempera
2. For operation on a dry, grass runway, increase distances (bot
"total to clear 50 ft. obstacle" figure.

—MAXIMUM RATE-OF-Cl

GROSS WEIGHT LBS.	AT SEA LEVEL & 59° F.			AT 5000 FT. & 41° F.		
	IAS, MPH	RATE OF CLIMB FT. /MIN.	FUEL USED, GAL.	IAS, MPH	RATE OF CLIMB FT. /MIN.	FUEL USED FROM S.L.,GAL.
1600	76	670	0.6	73	440	1.6

2.6. Best angle of climb speed is most often indicated as "IAS 50 ft mph." (Cessna Aircraft Company; for illustration purposes only, not to be used for flight planning or aircraft operation) margin. But when flying behind some of the high-powered engines (say, over 250 HP), you *may* have a problem. You can hang some of these powerful planes right on the prop. A study of the manual may reveal that power-off stall speed nearly matches, or even *exceeds*, best angle of climb speed. Now, what would happen to the pilot flying at best-angle speed if the engine failed over the obstacle at, say, 100 feet? All I can say is that that pilot better be an ace.

If the plane you fly states a best-angle speed that offers no safe margin above the power-off stall speed, treat the short-field procedure as an emergency procedure. You would be well advised to wait until you have normal takeoff conditions at hand; wait for a better headwind or for the temperature to dwindle or lighten the load by defueling or ferrying passengers out one by one.

Best Rate of Climb Speed. By best rate of climb speed we mean that speed which, with proper climb power applied, gains the greatest altitude in the least amount of *time* flown, consistent with engine cooling. It is the speed we set our plane at after clearing obstacles. This speed is normally stated in the plane's rate-of-climb chart (Fig. 2.7).

It is important, both for the efficiency of the climb and the welfare of your engine, that we do indeed climb at best-rate speed. Some pilots feel that they save their engine with a flatter climb and higher speed, but this works the engine harder for a longer time. Others feel that a steeper climb at a lower speed gets them upstairs faster. This, however, only *adds* to the climb time. The additional time required to gain the altitude occurs because any airspeed lower than best-rate speed moves the plane toward the *region of reverse command,* also referred to as the *backside of the power curve.*

Let's take a moment to understand this region of reverse command. It refers to the plane's climb capability at various airspeeds. A couple of examples explain the concept. Picture yourself flying a small ship at its cruise speed of 100 knots at 2400 rpm. You decide to establish slow flight. To slow to 90 knots and maintain altitude, you reduce throttle to 2200 rpm and slightly raise the nose. To slow

ASSOCIATED CONDITIONS:

POWER	2700 RPM, FULL THR(OTTLE)
FLAPS	UP
GEAR	UP

SEA LEVEL			4000 FEET			8000 FE(ET)	
C	R/C FT/MIN	CLIMB SPEED MPH/KTS	OAT °F °C	R/C FT/MIN	CLIMB SPEED MPH/KTS	OAT °F °C	R/C FT/MI(N)
-7	988		20 -7	713		0 -18	494
4	937		40 4	668		20 -7	447
16	891	92/80	60 16	622	92/80	40 4	403
27	846		80 27	578		60 16	360
			100 38	536		80 27	317
7	1101		20 -7	814		0 -18	586
4	1048		40 4	767		20 -7	537
16	999	91/79	60 16	720	91/79	40 4	491
27	953		80 27	674		60 16	447
38	909		100 38	630		80 27	403

2.7. Best rate of climb speed is normally found in the climb performance chart. (Beech Aircraft Corporation; for illustration purposes only, not to be used for flight planning or aircraft operation)

further, to 80 knots, you again reduce power (say to 2000 rpm) and lift the nose a little higher. Another speed reduction to 70 knots calls for about 1800 rpm and even more pitch, and you still hold altitude. But when you make a final speed reduction to 60 knots, you suddenly need to add power to maintain altitude. You need *more* power to fly *slower*; you are flying in the region of reverse command. You also have only minimal climb ability. This happens because a plane's climb performance at any particular airspeed depends on the reserve power it still has, additional to that needed to hold altitude at that particular airspeed.

Here's another example of climb performance. Imagine your-self flying that same airplane at its top speed of 110 knots under full power. How much climb performance does your plane have at this speed? None. It needs all the power it can muster just to hold altitude at top speed. Now imagine yourself in that same plane, staggering nose high through the air at 50 knots with full power needed just to keep it in the air. How much climb ability does your plane have at this minimum speed? Again, none. Obviously some-where between the plane's maximum and minimum speeds lies the optimum climb speed, and this is best rate of climb speed.

FIELD ELEVATION. Field elevation plays a critical role in takeoff performance. We all know that. Many pilots who have done most of their training and flying from airports near sea level don't understand just *how* critical, however. For example, it is not un-usual for a light plane to need 50 percent more distance when departing a 5000-foot-high mountain airport. Add to this the fact that many of these planes suffer a 30 percent loss of climb ability after the wheels leave the ground.

The thinner air of high altitude is, of course, responsible for the lower performance and extra distance needed. This thin air adversely affects takeoff performance in three ways:

1. Reduced lifting capability of the wings.
2. Reduced engine output.
3. Erroneous airspeed reading.

Reduced Lift. The air is thinner at high altitude simply because the reduced atmospheric pressure allows the molecules of air to spread out. With the molecules farther apart, the wing has to travel faster through them to get the same mass of air flowing over the airfoil. This faster speed translates into a longer ground run needed to accelerate to flying speed.

Reduced Engine Output. Thin air also reduces the engine's per-formance. The horsepower that the engine delivers to the prop is dependent on how much fuel we feed to the cylinders—but in a proper air-to-gasoline mixture. Light-aircraft engines are designed to run on a 15:1 ratio of air to gasoline. This means that the thinner air requires us to lean the mixture for a high-altitude take-off. Since it is the gasoline that holds the energy and since leaning cuts down the amount, our engine delivers less power. If the high elevation is not high *enough* to justify leaning for takeoff, the moderately thin air produces an overrich mixture that costs power. Either way, this reduction in power adversely affects our rate of acceleration to flying speed as well as our climb performance away from the ground.

Erroneous Airspeed Reading. The thinner air of high altitude affects the air's impact on the pitot tube in much the same manner that it affects the flow of air mass across the wing. You must fly faster to get the same impact. This means that there is a difference between the speed you are *actually* flying and what the airspeed indicator *says* you are flying, the difference between *true airspeed* (TAS) and *indicated airspeed* (IAS). At higher altitudes the plane is actually flying faster than the airspeed indicator says. A good rule of thumb figures the difference: to estimate true airspeed, add 2 percent to indicated airspeed for each 1000 feet above sea level.

But let me say here that when facing a mountain-airport take-off, adhere to the manufacturer's indicated sea-level airspeeds for both rotate speed and climb speed. Do this because thin air affects both the airspeed indicator and the wings in the same manner. Thus, if the manufacturer recommends sea-level indicated 60 knots for lift-off, then rotate at the 5000-foot field elevation at the 60 knots indicated. And if a 65-knot indicated best angle of climb speed is called for at sea level, then use it to clear those mountain obstacles. Just remember that your 60-knot indicated has you breaking away at true airspeed of 66 knots (5000 @ 2%/1000 = 10%; 10% × 60 = 6; 60 + 6 = 66). This means a longer ground run is needed to get there. By the same token, if 65 knots is stated for best angle of climb, then fly that speed on your airspeed indicator. Just know that the true airspeed of 71 knots produces a faster ground travel which requires more distance to the obstacle.

These three factors—diminished lift, reduced power, erroneous airspeed reading—combine to require a greater distance to safely depart a high-elevation airport.

RUNWAY TEMPERATURE. Temperature has the same effect on takeoff performance as does field elevation. And for the same good reason; any increase in runway temperature drives the molecules of air farther apart—it produces thin air. The results are much the same as we experience at high elevations: TAS increases slightly over IAS, the wings have fewer molecules of air to grab, the engine loses performance.

Many takeoff charts predicate takeoff performance at various field elevations against only "standard-day temperature" for those elevations (Fig. 2.8). Representative standard-day temperatures are

Sea level: 59°F
2500-foot field elevation: 50°F
5000-foot field elevation: 41°F
7500-foot field elevation: 32°F

To estimate standard-day temperature for your particular field elevation, simply use 59°F at sea level as a base and subtract 4°F for each 1000 feet of field elevation. Then, if the performance chart does not account for *actual* temperature, apply a rule of thumb: increase takeoff distance by 10 percent for every 20 degrees F above "standard" for the field elevation.

When calculating the takeoff distance from a short strip, determine the runway temperature. During your preflight inspection, make note of the reading on your outside temperature gauge sticking throught the windscreen. Remember that if the runway is paved and you are parked on the grass, you had better add a few degrees to the temperature indicated.

A combination of high field elevation and warm temperature seriously affects takeoff performance. As an example, the flight manual for a popular four-placer gives sea-level standard-day dis-

TAKE-OFF DA

TAKE-OFF DISTANCE WITH 20° FLAPS FROM H

GROSS WEIGHT LBS.	IAS @ 50' MPH	HEAD WIND KNOTS	AT SEA LEVEL & 59°F.		AT 2500 FT. & 50°F.		
			GROUND RUN	TOTAL TO CLEAR 50' OBS	GROUND RUN	TOTAL TO CLEAR 50' OBS	
2950	63			1350	845	1625	
			490	1025	595	1245	
			310	740	385	910	
		0	485	955	575	1120	
		10	325	710	395	840	
		20	195	490	245	590	
	52	0	295	655	350	745	
		10	185	460	225	530	
		20	105	305	130	355	

NOTES: 1. Increase distances 10% for each 25°F above standard temperature f
2. For operation on a dry, grass runway, increase distances (both "gro obstacle") by 7% of the "total to clear 50 ft. obstacle" figure.

2.8. Many charts convert standard-day conditions to representative elevations. (Cessna Aircraft Company; for illustration purposes only, not to be used for flight planning or aircraft operation)

tance required of 1525 feet. But at a field elevation of just 2500 feet at 85°F, that figure jumps to 2250 feet—pretty tight for, say, a 3000-foot strip.

Both field elevation and temperature affect takeoffs more than they affect landings. it makes sense. After all, when landing we are not dependent on maximum power and we're coming down anyway. The combination of high field elevation and warm temperature gives credibility to mountain-pilot Gerry's question to the city-airport pilot: "Don't you know you can get the plane into a place you can't get out of?"

HEADWIND COMPONENT. Plain logic tells us that a headwind shortens both the ground run and our climb distance to the obstacle. A 10-knot direct headwind, for example, already has our wing "flying" at 10 knots even before we start rolling. And this "gives" us 10 knots less that we must accelerate to, to reach flying speed. This, of course, means less ground run to get there. Once the plane is airborne the headwind reduces our ground speed toward the obstacle, giving us several additional seconds of climb for those extra feet of altitude.

While nearly all takeoff charts relate the headwind component to takeoff distance, many do not tell how to convert the existing crosswind to a direct headwind component (Fig. 2.9). You must

NORMAL TAKE-OFF DISTANCE

ASSOCIATED CONDITIONS: NOTES:

POWER	2700 RPM, FULL THROTTLE	1. FOR EA(
MIXTURE	LEAN TO FIELD ELEVATION	REDUCE
FLAPS	15°	AND TAI
GEAR	RETRACTED, AFTER LIFT—OFF	2. RATE OF
RUNWAY	PAVED, LEVEL, DRY SURFACE	AT TAKE
WEIGHT	2750 LBS	AND AT
TAKE—OFF SPEEDS	LIFT—OFF 71 MPH/62 KTS IAS	3. WHERE T
	50 FT 75 MPH/65 KTS IAS	BEEN DE
		AFTER L

WIND COMPONENT DOWN RUNWAY KNOTS	SEA LEVEL			2000 FT			4000	
	OAT °F °C	GROUND ROLL FEET	TOTAL OVER 50 FT OBSTACLE FEET	OAT °F °C	GROUND ROLL FEET	TOTAL OVER 50 FT OBSTACLE FEET	OAT °F °C	GROUN ROLL FEET
0	20 -7	1003	1544	20 -7	1172	1837	20 -7	1374
	40 4	1087	1674	40 4	1269	1996	40 4	1485
	60 16	1174	1812	60 16	1370	2166	60 16	1601
	80 27	1265	1957	80 27	1474	2346	80 27	1721
	100 38	1359	2108	100 38	1590	2559	100 38	1845
15	20 -7	781	1258	20 -7	922	1510	20 -7	1090
	40 4	851	1370	40 4	1003	1648	40 4	1185
	60 16	924	1489	60 16	1088	1797	60 16	1283
	80 27	1001	1615	80 27	1176	1955	80 27	1385
	100 38	1080	1747	100 38	1267	2127	100 38	1491

2.9. Most charts leave the calculations of headwind component up to the pilot. (Beech Aircraft Corporation; for illustration purposes only, not to be used for flight planning or aircraft operation)

make the conversion yourself. To evaluate the wind direction and velocity, look to the wind sock. First, estimate the angle that the wind crosses the runway. Normally, that sock won't stand perfectly still for you to do so—wind rarely blows constant. But try to average out the direction over a period of several seconds. Then determine the wind's velocity. Wind socks are designed to stiffen at 15 knots. So, a sock with a one-third droop indicates 10 knots. If the droop has the sock at a 45-degree angle, velocity is 7 or 8 knots. If it hangs with a two-thirds droop, you have about 5 knots. Once you know how the wind angles across the runway and you know its velocity, convert a crosswind to its direct headwind component. If the sock is swinging within 30 degrees of runway alignment, consider it a direct headwind. Allow half the wind's velocity as a headwind component when the sock swings 30 degrees to 60 degrees off the runway. And when the sock's angle with the runway exceeds 60 degrees, count the headwind zero (Fig. 2.10).

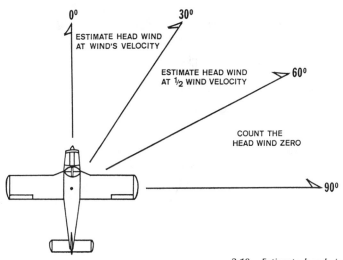

2.10. *Estimate headwind component by relating wind velocity to the angle at which the wind blows across the runway.*

AIRCRAFT LOADING. The more an airplane weighs, the greater the inertia an engine must overcome as it accelerates toward flying speed. Ground run is lengthened. Once the plane is off, climb performance suffers as that engine pulls its load uphill.

Most takeoff charts specify distances for various gross weights (Fig. 2.11). A few do not. These charts may only show distance required at the plane's *maximum allowable* gross weight. In these cases apply a rule of thumb for lightly loaded takeoffs: reduce the required distance by 5 percent for each 100 pounds below maximum allowable gross weight.

TAKE-

TAKE-OFF DISTANCE WITH

GROSS WEIGHT LBS.	IAS @ 50' MPH	HEAD WIND KNOTS	AT SEA LEVEL & 59°F. GROUND RUN	TOT				
2950	63	0			845		1625	
		10		1025	595		1245	
				740	385		910	
2500	58	0	485	955	575		1120	
		10	325	710	395		840	
		20	195	490	245		590	
2000	52	0	295	655	350		745	
		10	185	460	225		530	
		20	105	305	130		355	

NOTES: 1. Increase distances 10% for each 25°F above standard temperatur
2. For operation on a dry, grass runway, increase distances (both "g obstacle") by 7% of the "total to clear 50 ft. obstacle" figure.

2.11. Some charts contemplate only "maximum allowable" gross weight. Others state performance at various loadings. (Cessna Aircraft Company; for illustration purposes only, not to be used for flight planning or aircraft operation)

Of course, the manufacturer's charts assume that your plane does not exceed the maximum weight allowed. In the case of over-weight takeoffs the manufacturer has no idea what will happen — you are suddenly a test pilot.

While nearly all takeoff charts discuss aircraft weight, I know of none that mention aircraft balance. Balance is so critical to takeoff safety that, again, the manufacturer assumes a properly loaded aircraft. Of course, grief does not come to all planes that take off slightly out of balance. It takes the onset of a stall to trigger a spin. Unfortunately most stall/spin accidents *do* occur during either the takeoff or landing phases of the flight. At low altitude, the pilot stands little chance of recovery.

A few examples may show how critical aircraft balance is to stall and spin recovery. ATC received a call several summers ago from a training flight over south Florida. The instructor on board radioed that he and the student (a commercial pilot seeking her CFI) planned a practice spin. They were at 5200 feet and expected to recovered by 3000. The plane was a popular four-place trainer. Moments after the initial call, ATC received another: "Mayday! Mayday! It won't come out." And it didn't. Several weeks later, over the same part of the state, a similar accident happened in a similar plane. In this one a high-time instructor was giving a student training in stall recovery. The plane stalled, spun, and didn't recover.

Investigations into both accidents revealed five startling facts that must make us stop and think. First, each plane had a profes-sional pilot aboard who was familiar with the aircraft. Second, each aircraft was a type commonly called "forgiving." Third, de-pending on how the plane was loaded, each aircraft fit either the *normal* or *utility* category, with spins approved only when loaded utility. Fourth, while each plane was properly loaded for normal category, each was loaded aft of utility limits. And fifth, each plane exeeded the aft utility limit by less than one-half inch. In-teresting, isn't it, just how critical balance can be — particularly immediately after lift-off when the plane is nose high at a slow speed close to the ground. Here's another example a bit closer to home. One of the trainers that I fly day in and day out is a garden variety two-seater. The plane is about as docile as they come. Yet with myself and a student of my weight aboard, full tanks, and the seat shoved aft to accommodate my big feet, the airplane is unsafe to fly. It is slightly over gross and just barely aft of limits, about a half-inch as a matter of fact.

To guard against the disastrous combination of improper balance and an inadvertent stall following takeoff, learn how to use your plane's weight and balance data. Some manual presentations are simple to use, others are not. If you are unsure about the graphs' procedures, have an instructor guide you through some sample loadings.

When should light-plane pilots calculate weight and balance prior to takeoff? As a rule of thumb, run a weight and balance calculation any time the seating capacity is over half-filled or when there is any baggage in the luggage compartment.

PILOT TECHNIQUE. Takeoff performance charts assume average pilot technique. Now, I don't know exactly what that term means. But I do know this: if your proposed flight encompasses a short-field takeoff and your short-field experience is minimal or your skills are rusty, the solution is clear—get some short-field training before you depart.

Your short-field technique should include certain elements.

Preflight Research. Before takeoff, carefully relate the performance charts to the takeoff variables at hand. Make note of recommended indicated airspeeds: rotate speed, best angle of climb speed, best rate of climb speed. Study the manufacturer's procedure for leaving a short field. Then carefully adhere to all recommended speeds and procedures. The manufacturer knows what works best for its airplane. Following that good advice, rather than hearsay pass-along advice of other pilots, is the only way to go.

Verify Engine Performance. Don't wait until you are rolling pell-mell down the runway to evaluate engine full-power performance. There is just too much noise, movement, and distraction. Rather, before the roll starts, make a full-power run-up. Look for the rpm's that you know should be there. Listen for suspicious hiccups. Carburetor ice is a common culprit. If you are departing a mountain airport in excess of a 5000-foot elevation, now is the time to lean for maximum performance.

Use All the Runway. In many cases the taxiway enters the runway several yards up from the threshold. Don't hesitate to back-taxi in order to gain every foot available.

Deliver Rapid Acceleration. Do everything you can to gain flying speed in the shortest possible distance. Proper tire inflation is a must. Don't rely on a visual pressure check; verify it with a tire gauge. Don't deflect the control surfaces unnecessarily. Don't let your toes rest on the brakes. Don't *jam* the throttle to overload the carburetor—a smooth push works fine. Acceleration is helped if you relieve some of the weight on the nosewheel with *slight* back pressure—not so much that you produce aerodynamic drag but just enough to let you *feel* the rolling friction lessen.

Some pilots enter the runway with a high-power taxi, then whip into runway alignment to gain a few yards. I'm against this. It's just too easy to tip the plane and tatter a wing tip—you would not believe how quickly it can happen.

Positive Rotation. As you reach rotate speed, apply positive back pressure. The plane will lift off just as advertised. Then once off, establish the pitch attitude that you know (from practice) produces the correct climb speed toward the obstacle and trim to that airspeed.

Flap Management. Most manuals that have you leaving a short field with flaps advise you to leave them extended until you clear the obstacle. With good reason. The manual often has you climbing at near flaps-up-stall-speed. A sudden flap retraction coupled with a moment's inattention to airspeed could produce a minimum-altitude stall. I like to leave the flaps extended until I gain 500 feet.

Quite apart from the facts, figures, and procedures of the plane's manual, there are two fail-safe measures that you may want to plan into your short-field takeoffs.

Fail-safe Measures

Prudent pilots put into place two fail-safe measures when planning a departure from a short runway. The first is intended to stop a potentially hazardous situation before it gets started. The second is designed to halt a bad takeoff once it gets under way but *before* it can lead to tragedy.

MINIMUM SAFE-RUNWAY DISTANCE. Even after carefully relating the performance chart to the takeoff situation at hand, mistakes can occur. And you might discover too late that the calculated distance is inadequate. Reasons for miscalculations abound: an unexpected patch of soft runway during the ground run, a headwind that dies during the roll or climbout, a simple mistake in arithmetic or in interpreting the chart, and many others. For these reasons and for the sake of safety, add a margin for error. Here's what I'd suggest. First, remember the total-to-clear-obstacle figure is of paramount value to the departing pilot. For safety's sake, apply a rule of thumb: do not even begin a takeoff unless the runway length provides 150 percent of this total distance for the prevailing conditions. As an example, consider a performance chart that demands a total-to-clear-obstacle distance of 1600 feet. Unless that runway exceeds 2400 feet (1600 × 1.5) or unless you are an ace, *don't* try it!

ABORT/STOP DISTANCE. Incorporate a fail-safe measure that practically guarantees that a dangerous takeoff, once started, can be safely stopped. Before you begin your takeoff from any short strip, determine a safe abort/stop distance and flag it with a marker alongside the runway. If your plane is not off by that point, you can abort the takeoff with very little risk of damage. Run beyond that point and you are committed. The plane *must* lift off or suffer damage. Very few single-engine light-airplane manuals state an abort/stop distance. I suggest a rule of thumb: if you runway has a safe 150 percent of the required total distance, then its midpoint should provide a safe abort/stop distance. To determine the absolute minimum safe abort/stop distance, look to the landing performance chart. Use 150 percent of the "landing roll" distance given for the runway conditions at hand (Fig. 2.12). (For a thorough understanding of landing performance, refer to Fowler, *Making Perfect Landings in Light Airplanes,* Iowa State University Press, 1984.)

LANDING DISTANCE ꓿

LANDING DISTANCE WITH 40° FLAPS ON HARD S

PPROACH IAS MPH	@ SEA LEVEL & 59° F		@ 2500 FEET & 50° F		@ 5000
	GROUND ROLL	TOTAL TO CLEAR 50 FT. OBS.	GROUND ROLL	TOTAL TO CLEAR 50 FT. OBS.	GROUN ROLL
69	590	1350	640	1430	680

ᴇS: 1. Dist   es shown are based on zero wind, power off and heavy bra
    2. R   landing distances 10% for each 5 knots headwind.
    3.   peration on a dry, grass runway, increase distances (both "g
                 cle") by 20% of the "total to clear 50 ft. obstacle" figure.

2.12. Figure abort/stop distance by reference to the landing data. (Cessna Aircraft Company; for illustration purposes only, not to be used for flight planning or aircraft operation)

To determine and mark this distance, you may need to taxi up the runway. Travel to a point where the runway distance looks equal in each direction. I recommend getting out of the plane at that point and marking the spot with a highly visible "flag" (a weighted sheet of paper or handkerchief works fine). Stop the takeoff if your wheels are still on the ground at that point. Then, decide whether you want to try it again or wait until wind or temperature favors a shorter roll.

When should a light-plane pilot put short-field calculations and procedures into play? I would say any time the runway is less than 3000 feet long and the elevation exceeds 2500 feet *or* the temperature exceeds 85°F.

So, there is a chapter of thoughts to consider when proposing a departure from a short runway. It does take considerable time and effort to plan a safe departure. But for the sake of your plane, yourself, and your passengers, there is no other way. To do otherwise is to depend on chance. The very nature of chance is that it must someday turn against us.

IN REVIEW: Short-Field Takeoffs

PREFLIGHT REMINDERS

- "Don't you know you can get into a place you can't get out of?"
- Tire inflation goes hand in hand with runway surface versus takeoff distance.
- Obstacles do not always come in standard FAA 50-foot heights.
- Leave flaps extended until all obstacles are cleared.
- Best angle of climb speed may not provide a safe margin over power-off stall speed in higher-powered airplanes.
- The thinner air of high-altitude airports reduces the wing's lift, impairs engine output, and causes erroneous airspeed readouts.
- The *indicated* airspeed that does the job at sea level also does the job at high altitudes.

- Takeoff chart distances assume the airplane is loaded within proper balance and is not over maximum allowable gross weight.
- Verify proper engine output with a full-power run-up before takeoff.
- Use all the runway; do not hesitate to back-taxi if necessary.
- Do not even begin a takeoff unless the runway provides 150 percent of the needed total distance to clear obstacles.
- Calculate a safe abort/stop distance and flag it with a marker.
- Put short-field calculations and procedures into play whenever the runway is less than 3000 feet long and the elevation exceeds 2500 feet or the temperature exceeds 85°F.

IN-FLIGHT AIDS

SHORT-FIELD RESEARCH

1. Runway surface: paved _____; unpaved _____; soft_____
2. Proper tire inflation: _____psi
3. Estimated obstacle height: _____ft
4. "Air distance" needed for each additional 50 feet of obstacle height: _____ft
5. Recommended flap setting: _____degrees
6. Recommended rotate speed: _____ kts/mph
7. Recommended best angle speed: _____kts/mph
8. Power-off stalling speed: _____kts/mph
9. Recommended best rate airspeed: _____kts/mph
10. Field elevation: _____ft
11. Runway temperature: OAT _____degrees F
12. Headwind component: _____kts
13. Aircraft loaded weight: _____lb
14. Aircraft maximum allowable gross weight: _____lb (Balance verified?)
15. Charted distance required: _____ft
16. Extra distance for safety margin: _____ft
17. Abort/stop distance required: _____ft
18. Runway length available: _____ft
19. Total distance desired: _____ft

2.13. Relate accumulated information to the aircraft manual's takeoff performance chart and short-field procedure section.

CHAPTER THREE

Soft-Field Takeoffs

There is something about doing a soft-field takeoff that recalls of things past. Ghosts of deft Wacos and canvas-armored Spads and the *punchukata-puchukata* of climbing Kinner engines inhabit those fields that turn to mush after a summer's rain. Our minds allow a population: Charles Lindbergh, Amelia Earhart, Jimmy Doolittle. Immortality? Certainly. Others too—nameless, just like ourselves—seeking the simple joy that is flight, seeking entry to the airman's fraternity.

Does membership earned into this elite offer immortality? Yes, I think it most certainly does. And not just to those few pilots who are written of in the annals. Immortality is also extended to the thousands of aviators who remain unrenowned. For it is the most valiant efforts of these unnamed flyers that reach down the airways to enter our cockpits, to touch *our* flying. Certainly our mind's imprint of the faceless bush pilot allows him entry to our cockpit. We think of him, somewhere in time, skimming the tundra beneath the rapidly lowering overcast, searching, desperate for a firm, landable patch of survival. Or we think of a long-forgotten mission pilot, urging her fuel-starved Stinson across the lifeless, arid Kalahari to meet the medical needs of those suffering at the other end. We think of these pilots and we sit a little straighter at the controls, and we bear down a little harder. Just as our efforts are also spurred by the knowledge that some time in the past a nameless airmail pilot found himself, tired to numbness, flying alone through the snow-laced night, peering downward from his de-Havilland's cockpit, searching for — often imagining — the field's dim beacon that means success and sleep.

Our expertise meets theirs. The span of years is of little consequence. We are of their mettle, they are of ours — pilots are pilots. We try, as we must, to make our own flying worthy of their ghostly appraisals. But of even greater importance, our flying must also be worthy of the pilots who are to follow us, who will draw from *our* efforts. Because, just as sure as Champion makes little ceramic spark plugs, some summer day in 2095 weekend pilots are going to be tooling along at 40,000 feet in their Cessna Skyhawk XXXVIs, and they are going to think of us. They will punch London into their Collins, feed it their flight-profile disc, and think of you and me bashing through weather with hand-flown plane and handheld chart. That pilot will sit a little straighter at the controls and try a little harder, to be worthy of *our* ghostly appraisals. In turn, that pilot will leave something worthwhile for the pilots yet to follow. Immortality? Certainly! But our flying must be good enough to keep the chain unbroken.

There is a reason that flying fields with a tendency toward softness are inhabited with the ghosts of yesteryear's planes. Those planes were designed with soft fields in mind. Yesterday's high-stepping Travel Airs and Wacos sported tailwheels that held props high and away from danger (Fig. 3.1). Even at taxi speed, the uptilted wings provided lift. And those big main tires might have been yanked from the axle of a Model T. They just levered themselves through the mud and ruts with each rotation.

Modern light planes, on the other hand, require a special technique for getting out of soft fields. Today's engines, props, and wings are more than adequate for the job. Certainly they are more efficient than those of yesterday's planes. With today's typical light plane, it is the underpinnings that cause the soft-field problem. Today's little space-saving tires are just the right size to drop into

3.1. Planes of yesterday
sported large tires and a
tailwheel that produced an
angle of attack that helped
the pilot through the soft
spots.

any mud hole that comes their way. The tricycle gear carries us level, with the prop close to the ground picking up clods. The nosewheel wants to plow ahead through the rough. We need a technique, then, that simulates a tailwheel and big tires that lift over the mud.

Basic Concepts

In order to simulate tailwheel rigging, conduct your ground travels with generous back pressure on the yoke. This provides two positive influences to the soft-field takeoff. First, it raises the propeller arc a few inches higher from the dips and bounces of a soft or rough surface. Second, it tips the wings upward for a few extra degrees in the angle of attack. It helps lift the main gear over the mud as it pulls the nosewheel out of the mire.

Left slogging through the mud, the plane may *never* accelerate to flying speed. Therefore, we may need to *force* the plane off the ground *below* flying speed. Then, once airborne, accelerate to flying speed. We can get away with this because of a phenomenon called *ground effect*. Any time that a wing develops lift, it produces wing-tip vortices (Fig. 3.2). These vortices are a principal source of aerodynamic drag. If we could eliminate them, we would appreciably reduce drag. This drag reduction *does* occur when we fly very close to the ground. The close proximity of the ground prevents vortex development (Fig. 3.3). The wings are then highly efficient and the plane will fly at a speed slightly lower than normal lift-off speed.

There is one sour note, however. If we allow the plane to climb

3.2. Wing-tip vortices form as a swirl of air that creates drag.

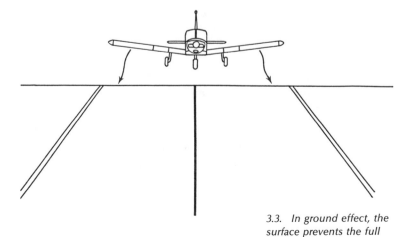

3.3. In ground effect, the surface prevents the full vortex from forming.

out of ground effect and regain drag at that slow speed, it may stall. Therefore, immediately after the wheels break away, we must keep the plane skimming level until we accelerate to normal rotate speed. (Ground effect, by the way, is effective up to about 12 feet in most light planes.)

All of this—soft ground, excessive back pressure, delayed acceleration—costs distance. This extra distance is both appreciable and unpredictable. Therefore, we need a fail-safe measure, and here's how to get it. First calculate the manual's total-to-clear-obstacle distance. Now, since much of the acceleration takes place *after* the wheels leave the ground, figure your required distance *from that point.* By example, let's say that the plane's manual calls for a total-to-clear-obstacle distance of 1600 feet. Let's also say that the soft strip has a published length of 3200 feet. We would then want to plan our abort/stop flag at about the runway's midpoint. Then, if we were not airborne by that point, we would abort the takeoff.

Soft-Field Technique

If the infield or taxiway is as soft as the runway, begin your soft-field procedure while still in the ramp area. Perform your takeoff checks and run-up right there (beware your propwash). Once taxiing, you may not want to stop. Do not, however, attempt to run your checks while busy taxiing. To do so invites an accident.

Taxi with full back pressure on the yoke and with enough power to slow-taxi through the soft surface. The extra power that pulls you through the mush produces a mild prop blast across the upward deflected elevator and helps diminish the nosewheel's drag across the ground. Unless the manual states otherwise, taxi with the flap extension suggested by the manufacturer for short-field departures. This partial extension usually produces the best lift/drag ratio. Once under way, try to avoid stopping; plan to roll right into the takeoff run. Plan ahead and try to taxi around the very softest or roughest patches. If there is a mushy area that you cannot detour, be ready to increase power slightly to maintain a constant taxi speed. When increasing throttle, however, it is best not to exceed 2000 rpm. Higher power often produces an erratic taxi that can damage the gear or dip the prop to the turf.

Should you let the plane come to a stop on a very soft surface, you may not get it rolling again without assistance. If you do get stuck, don't try to "gun" the plane out with power while passengers push on struts and wing tips. During the confusion of engine noise, prop blast, and an eagerness to help, someone is very apt to forget those invisible spinning blades. Also, a misdirected shove on a struct can cause damage as costly as the price of a new Chevrolet. Rather, go get a tow bar, tractor, and boards to put under the wheels.

Once you reach the runway, keep your plane rolling right into the takeoff run. Start your run with the yoke full aft to lighten the nosewheel load as soon as possible. Once speed increases, you will find that full-aft stick pressure produces *excessive* pitch, enough to actually retard acceleration. So, relax some yoke pressure. Keep just enough back pressure to let you feel the nosewheel skim the surface. This moderate back pressure is also the amount that helps lift the main gear across the soft surface. In short, you simulate yesteryear's tailwheel rigging and high-lifting wheels.

With the yoke aft, the plane should lift away before it reaches normal rotate speed. As it does so, slightly lower the nose to keep the plane from climbing out of ground effect. Let the airspeed increase to normal rotate speed, then pitch to the desired climb speed.

Practice your soft-field takeoff until you're good, really good. Then plan a ghost flight. Plan the flight for the mud time of early spring. Plan to avoid the victor airways that have never seen the wings of a Travel Air or a Curtis Robin or even a leather helmet. Seek out only those off-airway turf fields that show as hollow magenta symbols on the sectional. Evaluate them for reasonable lengths but pack a toothbrush just in case you have to delay your departure until a drying sun shines. Get the belly of your ship muddy. Fly back in time, join the fraternity, and say hello to a few immortal ghosts.

IN REVIEW: Soft-Field Takeoffs

PREFLIGHT REMINDERS

- Yesterday's tailwheel airplanes with high tires were designed with soft fields in mind.
- Today's tricycle gear and small tires lend difficulty to soft-field operations.
- Generous back pressure on the yoke raises the prop and nosewheel away from the ground; it helps lift the tires through a soft surface and simulates tailwheel rigging.
- Use ground effect to help the plane lift off at a slower-than-normal speed.
- Keep the plane in ground effect until it accelerates to safe flying speed.
- The extra distance needed to clear a soft field is difficult to determine.
- Plan an abort/stop point that considers the fact that much of the needed acceleration occurs after lift-off.
- Consider performing your pretakeoff checks while still in the ramp area.
- Plan ahead to keep your taxi speed constant.
- Start the takeoff run with full-aft yoke.
- As speed increases, relax enough yoke pressure to allow the nosewheel to skim the surface.
- The plane will lift off below normal rotate speed.
- Once off and normal rotate speed is attained, pull away from ground effect with the pitch attitude that delivers best rate of climb speed.

IN-FLIGHT AIDS

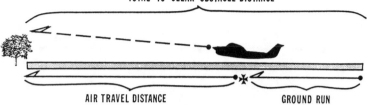

3.4. *Since much of the plane's acceleration occurs after lift-off, mark an abort/ stop distance that allows sufficient air-travel distance.*

The highest art form of all is a human being in control of himself and his airplane in flight, urging the spirit of a machine to match his own.

– Richard Bach
A Gift of Wings

CHAPTER FOUR

Critical Takeoff Situations

Every once in a while, a takeoff situation presents one or two
elements that we might call critical. Not emergency situations,
really, just critical—unless of course the critical element catches the
pilot unaware. *Then* the merely critical can quickly become emergency. Let's look at some of these situations in the light of "critical
only." Then, should they come our way, we are prepared to keep
them from becoming "emergency."

Wake Turbulence

Time was, we thought wake turbulence was due to "propwash." That was in the days of the DC-3. Its two radial
engines seemed to give our Cubs and Taylorcrafts no end of trouble. Then came the four-engined DC-4. Sure enough, more wake
turbulence, and even the Bonanzas and Mooneys had trouble.
Finally came the jets. No more propellers, no more propwash.
Things will improve, we thought. But things got worse! Now, even
the Barons and Navajos had to be beware of the turbulence. Something was wrong. Of course, we quickly learned that wake turbulence is *not* a result of propwash. Rather, it is a result of wing-tip
vortices.

Every airplane, even the smallest, generates wake turbulence.

The heavier the plane, however, the greater that turbulence. Wake turbulence is a by-product of *lift*. Lift is created by a pressure differential over the upper wing surface, while higher pressure develops under the wing. This difference in pressures—as the *high* wants to fill the *low*—triggers a swirl of air at each wing's tip (Fig. 4.1). Once these swirls are created, they remain intact as two counterrotating vortices trailing behind each wing.

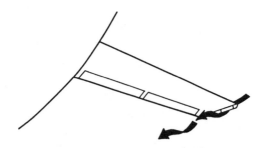

4.1. *Wing-tip vortices form as the air passing beneath the wing swirls upward to balance the upper-surface lower pressure.*

The rotational strength of these vortices can be dangerous to small planes. Even behind medium-size jetliners the vortex can rotate in excess of 100 knots—far more than the typical light plane's ailerons can deliver as counterroll. The turbulence is not usually great enough to damage your plane once airborne. But it *can* distract surprised pilots to the point that *they* do the damage.

We really don't want to become involved with these vortices as we share airports with large airplanes. Avoiding wake turbulence is made simpler if we understand the behavior of wing-tip vortices:

1. Since a vortex is a by-product of lift, wing-tip vortices are produced only when the wing is developing lift. Once the landing plane's tires touch, the vortices cease. Until the departing plane lifts off, vortices are nonexistent.

2. Wing-tip vortices, while remaining intact, begin sinking the moment they leave the wing tips. They generally settle at about 500 feet per minute, to a point 1000 feet below the large plane. At that point they level out. If you are departing below a jet or other heavy aircraft landing at another airport, there is usually little to worry about. Their final approach path is usually well above you. But if that liner is approaching to an intersecting runway at *your* airport, you may have a problem.

3. Vortices drift. Once the vortices from a departing or arriving plane settle to the ground, each vortex drifts outward. This ground travel is slow—about 5 knots—but vortices remain significant for about 1500 feet of lateral drift. Additionally, vortices drift with the wind. Either form of drift could present a problem to a light aircraft departing on a parallel runway.

4. Wake turbulence dissipates with time. About 3 to 4 minutes does the job, even on a calm day. Wind helps break them up, and even a 10-knot breeze halves their lift-span. If you are waiting at runway's end and are unsure about the vortices' estimated time of death, use my friend Moe's time-tested procedure. Just yield the right-of-way to that little 152 holding behind you. If *that* tiny ship makes it off OK, then fine, proceed with your takeoff.

5. Wing-tip vortices are relatively small in diameter; each is about 100 feet across. If you should encounter turbulence after lift-off, a heading change of several degrees (preferably upwind) should quickly fly you out of it.

Avoiding Wake Turbulence

With the characteristics of wing-tip vortices in mind, let's look at a few typical takeoff situations and see how we can best avoid wake turbulence.

Situation 1: Taking off behind a large plane that is either landing or executing a practice low approach. Allow at least 2 minutes for the turbulence to dissipate before taking off.

Situation 2: Taking off behind a departing large aircraft. Make note of the large plane's point of lift-off. If you can be off before that point, go ahead. Then, after lift-off alter your heading a few degrees upwind. Take care to avoid any subsequent turns that would cross the large plane's departure path.

Situation 3: Intersecting runways. If the departing or arriving flight path of the larger plane crosses your proposed runway, wait at least 2 minutes. If only that plane's ground roll crosses your runway, simple jet blast *may* be a problem. Wait 1 minute.

Situation 4: Parallel runway. If the parallel runway is within 2000 feet, you may get some of the drift. A crosswind makes the turbulence's position unpredictable. Wait 2 minutes.

Jets present another problem that goes hand in hand with wake turbulence. They give us jet-engine blast. The exhaust stream from a running jet engine can be a serious threat to light airplanes. Here are some rules of thumb for minimum separation to help avoid jet-blast turbulence in excess of 30 knots.

	Idle Power	*Breakaway Power*	*Takeoff Power*
Corporate-size jet	100 feet	200 feet	400 feet
Midsize jet	200 feet	400 feet	800 feet
Heavy jet	400 feet	800 feet	1600 feet

Should you find yourself sharing the run-up area with jets, take a few precautions against jet blast.

1. Stay away from runway's edge. Jet-engine exhaust drifts with the wind.
2. If a jet already occupies the run-up area, park well clear of breakaway distance. Try to anticipate the jet's next move and streamline your plane into the direction of possible blast.
3. When taxiing behind a jet, maintain a breakaway distance. You never know when the pilot may want to accelerate the taxi. Or the pilot may stop, then need breakaway power to get rolling again, and if you're too close, no amount of body English is going to throw your plane into reverse.

4. Let's say a jet pulls into the run-up area after you are parked. The pilot's mind is somewhere else and he either parks the plane too close or aims the tail at you. Don't hesitate to reposition — quickly. If other planes prevent repositioning and you and that jet are sharing ground control frequency, do not hesitate to holler at him.

Mountain-Airport Takeoffs

In the mountains, our takeoffs are often disturbed by factors other than the density altitude (combined field elevation and temperature) mentioned in a previous chapter. Other conditions we often must deal with are a very capricious wind and terrain slope. I have stood at a mountain airport and watched the wind sock at one end of the runway hang limp, while the sock at the other end swings stiff with a 90-degree crosswind.

Some mountain airports have a one-way runway; that is, take-offs are always made downhill on the sloping runway. The question might arise, Should I take off uphill into the wind or downhill with the wind at my tail? On a one-way strip there *is* only one way: you must take off downhill even if downwind. Let me add that the runway gradient is seldom the real problem here. Almost always it is the *terrain* at the upcountry end of the airport that stops the whole action. Your wheels may leave the ground when they are supposed to. You may climb after a fashion. But from a one-way strip, you may not be able to climb fast enough to clear the up-sloping terrain at the upcountry side of the airport.

Another question might arise, How much tailwind can I accept when departing a one-way airport? Look at your plane's take-off performance chart for an answer. First find the no-wind total distance to clear for the prevailing runway situation. Then apply a rule of thumb: add 20 percent to that distance for each 5 knots of tailwind component. Thus if your plane requires 2350 feet to achieve a 50-foot altitude for the field elevation, temperature, and loading, it would need at least 3290 feet with a 10-knot tailwind (plus, of course, the usual 50 percent margin for safety).

Tailwind takeoffs need a lot of room for two reasons. First, with the wind behind you, you use considerable ground run just to get the wings and propeller in "zero wind." *Then* you need the manual's distance to further accelerate to flying airspeed. Second, once off, the tailwind has you at a higher-than-normal ground speed. You travel the air distance quickly. If, after your rule-of-thumb estimate, you are still in doubt, apply another rule of thumb: don't go. Simply delay your takeoff until the wind shifts.

In the mountains, wind can affect safety during the climb-to-altitude phase of your takeoff. Nearby mountain peaks and ridges may funnel the wind to produce damaging mountain turbulence. When this occurs, it is not unusual to have winds with twice the velocity of nearby reporting stations. Expect this turbulence to exist if your airport is within 10 miles downwind from the mountain range. Downdrafts predominate in the flow of this turbulence, and the downdrafts can be stronger than your plane's climb performance. A good rule of thumb to follow is this: if stations near the mountains are reporting winds aloft in excess of 30 knots at mountaintop altitudes, postpone your departure until the winds subside. In general, mountain winds do not get bad until about 10:00 A.M., when the heat starts to build. The day's winds generally begin to weaken after 5:00 P.M., when the air begins to cool. Don't take off so late in the day, however, that darkness catches you over the mountains. Night flight over mountains in a single-engine light plane is risky business.

Your mountain-airport takeoff will be less critical if two facts are in evidence. First, make sure your plane has the performance. A study of the takeoff and climb charts before you even head for the mountains is in order. Compare expected performance against the expected environment as indicated by the sectional chart, weather forecast for the mountain area, and airport notations in the *Airport/Facility Directory.*

Second, your mountain takeoff will be made less critical with pilot experience. If you are a flatland pilot planning to head for the hills, get together with an instructor for some mountain takeoff training before you leave. Prepare for those conditions you will meet in the high country. On a windy day learn how to handle your plane on a narrow runway in gusty crosswinds. You and the instructor load a passenger or cases of engine oil aboard to simulate your expected loading. Maybe try a tailwind takeoff.

Handicap your takeoff to see what you and your plane can deliver on a high-density-altitude departure. Restrict your takeoff power by 75 rpm for each 1000 feet of field elevation that you wish to simulate. Thus, if your engine normally turns 2500 rpm on the takeoff run, restrict power to 2275 rpm to simulate a hot field 3000 feet higher than your home airport. Try to imagine a 500-foot ridge 2 miles out as your plane struggles for altitude. Obviously, you want to conduct this dual instruction from a *long* runway with no obstacles ahead. And you want to keep your throttle hand limber, just in case the action becomes too uncomfortable.

This simulation will provide realism. But there is a void between *realism* and *reality.* How narrow or how wide that void is, I cannot say with certainty. Therefore, I suggest a final precaution when flying toward that mountainous area. Land at an airport just short of the range. Get together with a local instructor for an hour of training and advice about the mountain area that you plan to fly through.

Then, with the facts in hand, recent training, and a plane of demonstrated capability, you should have no trouble with mountain-airport takeoffs.

A Minor Annoyance

There is one situation that sooner or later nearly every pilot faces on takeoff. Not a *critical* situation, really, unless the pilot chooses to make it so. Sooner or later nearly every pilot has a door pop open during the takeoff run or initial climbout. Nothing bad happens in the light plane. But is it noisy! POW! WHOOOOOSH! The noise alone can spook an uninformed pilot into error. But flight characteristics remain virtually unaffected. The door just trails open 2 inches and no one can push hard enough to fall out. Only a minor annoyance—really. Not all pilots *know* that. A story? Sure. Draw your chair closer and I'll tell you what happened.

The story is not new, you've heard it before because unfortunately, nearly every airport has had a similar experience. Ian was the embodiment of every Irish ballad ever written. He stood 5 feet 5 inches and had a happy-go-lucky grin just as wide. With a shock of red hair and a gift of blarney, he had a ready friendship for all. Ian was (and remained) a good pilot.

A score-and-a-half years ago, Ian bought a nearly new, sleek, four-place retractable of 260 HP. State of the art. And it was indeed art—soft smoke-blue with burgundy striping, latest stuff stacked in the panel, genuine leather interior. It was the star of the ramp. Ian was proud, we all were proud.

Ian had just completed an hour's checkout in the craft and was ready for a solo hop. We watched him taxi out, discussing the marvelous deep-throated power, just how that funny tail really worked—stuff like that.

In the cockpit, at runway's end, Ian shoved in takeoff power. The acceleration, the crisp lift-off. Then, POW! WHOOOOOSH! Ian stiffened like a corpse. That tornado of wind spilling in just had to blow his ship apart! He *had* to get it down, right now! Unfortunately there wasn't enough runway left under him. But fortunately (or unfortunately) big Lake Barton was dead ahead.

Well, you guessed it. Even from the hangar, we could both see and hear that terrible splash. Ian was a good swimmer, but that beautiful ship sank like a punctured rubber raft.

If this minor annoyance should ever come your way, treat it as such. You have three easy options, depending on whether or not you are still on the runway when the door opens. If the door pops during the ground run with plenty of stopping distance ahead, the solution is simple. First, out of courtesy, quickly reassure your passenger: "It's OK. Nothing will happen." Then throttle back, exit the runway, close and *lock* the door, and grumble your way back for a second run while you try to convince your passenger to stay aboard for another go.

If the door opens after lift-off or with inadequate stopping distance ahead, continue with the takeoff. Then you have two options. You can either circle and land to close the door or climb to cruise altitude and do it there. The point is, don't wrestle with the door at low altitude. If you choose to climb to altitude with the door sprung open, nothing bad will happen. (If it is the right-hand door, however, the passenger may tend to gurgle a bit now and then. But that aside, the climb will be uneventful.) Cabin doors are sometimes difficult to close in flight. It will help relieve the pressure against it if you slow-fly and open a window or storm vent.

If either the baggage or cowl hatch opens in flight, you have only one option. You can't reach either from your position, and *don't even ask* the passenger to unstrap and crawl back to close the baggage hatch. You must return for a landing.

If it is the cowl hatch that is in question, you may have another minor annoyance as you return for landing. The slipstream may flutter the hatch door hard enough to do damage. If this happens, fly the plane in a *slight* slip to alter the slipstream. A few seconds with ailerons and rudder produces the right combination that lets the hatch lie flat. No problem.

As I said, Ian's unfortunate flight occurred many years ago. He never had another mishap. Last year, at the insistence of his loving family, Ian, aged seventy-six, gave up flying. I think it was a wise decision. *Slainthe Is Saol Agat!,* Ian.

Engine Failure on Takeoff

An engine failure on takeoff can be merely critical or a full-blown emergency. If the engine loses power during the roll or after rotation with plenty of stopping distance ahead, there is little trouble. If, however, the engine quits after lift-off with the airport already behind, the pilot faces a truly desperate emergency. Serious injury is a real prospect. There is usually only time for a few discrepancy checks: switch tanks, try each magneto in turn, advance the throttle, pull carb heat, enrich mixture. Then the tough question, Turn back to the airport or try for another spot? The answer is rarely clear-cut. There are no clear-cut guidelines to follow. This is because the situations are so varied: point and height of engine failure, characteristics of the plane, partial or total power loss, nature of the airport. And, there are so few pilots with personal experience to pass along.

There are some basic concepts for you to consider that will improve your chances if a forced landing from takeoff should ever come your way. The nature of these basic concepts falls within two statements.

1. Know your airplane.
2. Know your airport.

KNOW YOUR AIRPLANE. When must I land straight ahead and when do I have enough altitude to turn back? To the pilot facing a forced landing following takeoff, the answer lies in knowledge of the airplane. Most light planes will give *about* a mile of glide for each 1000 feet of altitude. Each 90 degrees of turn usually costs *about* 250 feet. But only practiced demonstration provides certainty. Let's set up three rules of thumb. Then let's have *you* modify them for the plane you fly. Make a trial, practical demonstration.

Rule 1. If the engine fails below 500 AGL, select the best area within 30 degrees of turn and a quarter-mile glide. To modify this rule for your airplane, conduct a practical demonstration. With an observer pilot on board to help spot traffic, fly to an airport that has light traffic and long runways. Approach the runway threshold at a 30-degree angle. Slow the plane to a speed that simulates best rate of climb speed and descend so that you reach the airport boundary about 300 AGL. As the runway nears, close the throttle and make the shallow turn to final. You will discover that even a shallow turn costs altitude. Modify rule number one to meet the capability of the plane you fly.

Rule 2. If the engine fails between 500 and 1000 AGL, select a landing spot that lies within a half-mile and 90 degrees of turn. To modify this rule to your plane, set up a demonstration. With an observer pilot aboard, fly to an uncongested airport with long runways. Approach the runway on a base leg in slow flight at 500 AGL. Close the throttle as you approach final, a half mile out. Turn toward the runway, gauge your plane's ability, and modify rule two.

Rule 3. If the engine fails above 1000 AGL and the airport boundary lies within a half mile, execute a turn and return to the field. This situation would occur, naturally, only when departing a *long* runway, or when making a downwind departure.

Again, with an observer pilot aboard and an uncongested airport beneath you, set up an exercise to modify this rule to the plane you fly. Overfly the runway at 1000 AGL at a slow-flight speed that approximates climb speed. When the airport boundary is a half mile behind, begin your simulated forced landing. Close the throttle, turn toward the airport, and decide if you could make it to an unobstructed area. Then, modify the rule to suit your airplane.

As you modify this rule, keep in mind the basic problem. Be careful that your modified rule does not risk overreaching the capabilities of your plane. Pilots who have attempted to turn back with insufficient altitude for the distance have either hit the ground while still in a turn or have tried to stretch the glide. Either is a setup for disaster. When a plane hits while turning, it usually catches a wing tip and cartwheels. A pilot who tries to stretch a glide often stalls, and a stall from even 50 feet is like falling off a four-story building. In either case, survival is doubtful.

KNOW YOUR AIRPORT. You will probably never experience a forced landing from takeoff. But should it ever happen, chances favor it happening at your home airport, the one you use most. For this reason study the departure paths with each takeoff. Survey those areas for possible landing sites. Conduct a similar survey of the airports you frequently visit and you eliminate a good measure of uncertainty from the unlikely event.

When you enter the pattern of an unfamiliar airport, remind yourself that you will soon be departing. So on the downwind leg, survey the departure path for likely spots. Then, should the engine fail when a turn-back is inadvisable, you have an idea where relative safety lies.

Someday you may need to land where *no* safety lies. Even the big-city airport usually offers a possible emergency site—a parking lot, expressway median, or lake. But occasionally there is nothing. You must then land where you cannot land.

If this nightmare ever comes my way, logic will tell me two things. First, it will tell me that at the very least I'm going to get hurt. Second, it will say that even though the engine may be dead, the rest of the plane certainly is not. I would still have elevators, ailerons, rudder, and flaps. I would use that control as well as I could to come out alive. I'd put a three-part landing procedure into play.

1. I would aim for a spot that would let me avoid hitting anything solid with the nose. I wouldn't care about the *rest* of the plane, but I'd want to keep the cabin more or less intact.
2. My approach would be at the slowest possible speed, full flaps. Yet, I'd not let those wings stall; I wouldn't want to fall that last 50 feet.
3. I would not throw in the towel. Even if it continued to look hopeless, I'd keep working right up to the last moment, even *into* that last moment because the deciding factor may lie within that last instant of aircraft control.

There is, of course, an even bigger question at stake. There is the question of the occupants' welfare versus that of the people on the ground. That question is answerable only by the pilot if, and when, the unavoidable choice must be made.

IN REVIEW: Critical Takeoff Situations

PREFLIGHT REMINDERS

- Wing-tip vortices are produced only when the wing is providing lift.
- Wing-tip vortices sink to a point 1000 feet below the large airplane.
- Vortices drift outward for about 1500 feet.
- On a calm day, vortices will dissipate in about 3 to 4 minutes; a 10-knot breeze halves their life span.
- Wing-tip vortices are about 100 feet in diameter.
- Departing after large airplane lands: delay 2 minutes.
- Departing behind a departing large airplane: either plan an early lift-off or delay departure.
- Intersecting runways: wait at least 2 minutes.
- In the run-up area, park well clear of a jet's breakaway distance.
- Maintain breakaway distance when taxiing behind the large airplane.
- Departing from a parallel runway: remember that vortices drift with the wind.
- On mountain airports, adhere to the direction of a one-way strip.
- You can expect mountain turbulence to exist 10 miles downwind from the ridge.
- A late departure that will have you still over the mountains in darkness is risky business.
- If inexperienced in mountain flying, get some training before you get to the mountains.
- Don't wrestle with an open door at low altitude.
- Survey the departure paths for emergency landing sites at both your home airport and those fields you frequently visit.

IN-FLIGHT AIDS

JET-BLAST AVOIDANCE

	Idle Power	*Breakaway Power*	*Takeoff Power*
Corporate-size jet	100 feet	200 feet	400 feet
Midsize jet	200 feet	400 feet	800 feet
Heavy jet	400 feet	800 feet	1600 feet

4.2. Approximate minimum separation to avoid jet blast in excess of 30 knots.

CHAPTER FIVE

Night Takeoffs

There is a pilot you must meet. You needn't travel far. Just go to the airport the first moonless, clear night that comes your way. Don't arrive until the beacon sweeps the ramped airplanes with strokes of green and white. Untie the plane to the accompaniment of airport night sounds — the cough of a distant engine coming to life, the rasp of an opening hangar door, the clack-clack of a prop coming to rest — all the sounds that are hidden by day.

Treat yourself to the clandestine adventure of a flashlit preflight. Poke the finger of light into the ship's dark corners and deep hidey-holes. Peer down under the cowl's hatch, past the whiff of mineral spirits. Search for the patch of dye that spells of gas dripping where it must not drip, the pool of oil that reveals a hidden leak, the white residue of a hairlined exhaust manifold. Seek out any lurking discrepancy that might breathe disaster into the night flight.

Climb aboard, throw the master, and listen to the panel say, It is time to go; the pilot you seek waits aloft. Blast the night quiet with a twist of the key. Taxi through the pinpoints of blue and solve the toughest navigation of all, getting from the ramp to the runway in the dark.

Draw up for your takeoff checks. Let the list guide your fingers through the darkened cockpit. Verify each instrument with a touch, each knob and handle with a confirming grab. Receive your "cleared for takeoff" from a hushed voice that implies a confidence to share, rather than a clearance in need of compliance.

Ease your plane into takeoff position exactly between the converging lines of glowing white dots. Push the throttle to the stop and watch dashes of center stripe accelerate through the oval patch of landing light. Plenty of runway—let the plane fly off and tune the trim for an easy climbout.

Bank away from the city lights. Climb through the rural blackness that cuts the cords of Earth. Level at cruise, steady the plane against a star centered in the windscreen, and trim for hands-off. Then, brighten the panel lights, look past your left shoulder to the face peering in, and meet yourself.

A remarkable encounter. Yet one so familiar to a *pilot*. Because a pilot's life aloft holds the needed catalyst, hours of solitude. Pilots expect to spend and enjoy many hours, quite alone, within the cockpit. Morning's flight might pass with only the company of the quilted farmlands drifting below. Afternoon may find the companionship of a building cumulus. And night flight may be shared with the sociability of glowing instruments.

Thus, a pilot's life aloft is not lived amid the clamor and clatter of Earth's woes that echo the failings of others: mutterings of greed, whimpers of the economic pendulum, shouts of impending doom. Pilots live free of those calamities that would drag them down. Worldly woes don't get much chance to clatter around within the cockpit, and you get a chance to meet yourself.

Chances are you will like the person you meet, for that pilot peering in possesses a self-reliance and independence that can crackle and flash within the cockpit. It is a temperament born of necessity because, as pilots, we engage in one of life's few remaining endeavors in which we are solely responsible for our own well-being. Once aloft, the pilot has left behind the battery of experts. Decisions must be made alone. The *pilot* must be the expert to analyze the faltering engine, to read the weather, to evaluate the risk. And when trouble enters, the outcome rests with that pilot alone. Pilots know, despite the promises of frequency labels, that help is *not* just 121.5 MHz away. Pilots know that when distress crawls aboard, the only meaningful help is right there in the cockpit, within the pilot's own skill, judgment, and knowledge. Any Mayday must be transmitted to that pilot's own self-reliance. Real practical help will come from no other source. That pilot peering in from the darkness beyond your left shoulder would have it no other way.

Hold your course steady toward that shimmering star that beckons a destination more likely than the winking beacon below. It is the stuff night skies are made of. No need to hurry the flight, the tanks are fat. Take time to enjoy the endless darkness of space—and the pleasure of your own company.

Basic Considerations of Night Takeoffs

Night takeoffs are not that much more difficult than daytime departures. They are just different. Yet the differences are great enough that we need to heed a few precautions. These precautions all relate to three simple facts of night takeoffs.

FACT 1. We simply don't see as well at night. Our eyes are constructed so that a nighttime blind spot lies in line with our direct forward vision. Our best night vision comes from an offset viewpoint, from the sides of our eyes. Yet, this viewpoint is difficult to maintain when we are busy with the mechanics of a takeoff.

Any reduction of oxygen in our blood, even from a cockpit made stuffy by passengers, seriously affects night vision. Toxic substances within the blood, such as nicotine or alcohol, are detrimental to night vision, as any smoker or pilot who has had a drink within the past 12 hours will tell you. Even age plays its part. The older we get, the more we must squint to read the Kollsman. In fact if you're in my age bracket (between fifty-five and death), you might even want to invite a younger pair of eyes along for the night flight.

FACT 2. Often what we *do* see at night is not always what it seems.

Night skies have their illusions. Illusions rank high as contributing factors of night-flying accidents. Take our perceptions of distance and time as an example. At night, distance appears compressed. What appears to be 5 miles is actually 10; what seems 100 feet is really 200 feet. And since our perception of time relies to an extent on the passing of landmarks, even minutes seem drawn out. What feels like 3 minutes might be only 1.

The points of light we do see at night often misinform. For example, a line of distant lights at an angle to our departure path can look like a sloping horizon (Fig. 5.1). It might make the nose seem too high and one wing low. Only the attitude indicator can tell for sure. A point of light abeam the airplane on initial climbout has its own lie to tell. If the plane's wings are banked toward the illumination when the pilot spots the light, it looks like the plane is too low, that it is not climbing (Fig. 5.2). Verification from the vertical speed indicator reveals the truth.

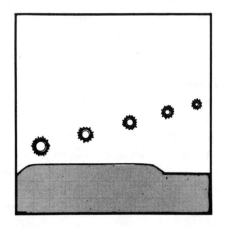

5.1. A line of distant lights at angles to the departure path can have the appearance of a sloping horizon.

Another example of ground lights fibbing to us? Say you are departing a runway over a void of dark terrain but with a light ahead in the distance. *If* you inadvertently let the nose rise, the angle from which you now see the light over the cowl makes it look like you are much higher than you really are (Fig. 5.3). Without

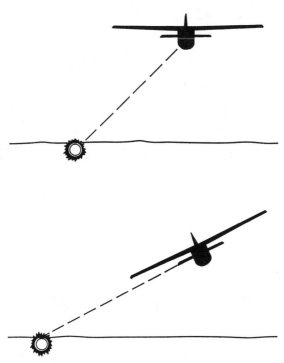

5.2. A pilot who notices an abeam point of light while the wings bank toward it can feel the illusion of being too low.

reference to the altimeter it could talk you into an early level off — not good if sloping terrain lies ahead. Even rain on the windscreen lets those ground lights deceive us. Refraction through the water on the windscreen bends the light much as it "bends" the soda straw in the glass of soft drink. It makes us look higher than the altimeter declares. Ground lights can even confuse our sense of direction when departing at night. During the day, we subconsciously use known landmarks or section lines to help guide our climbout. But at night the irregular patterns of ground lights are often confusing, and we need to know our desired headings and rely on the heading indicator to achieve them.

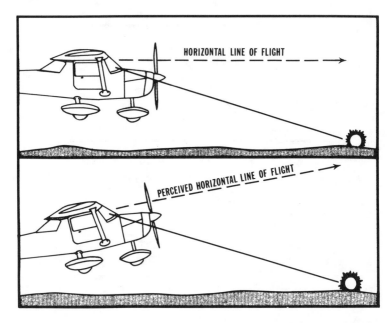

5.3. When unaware that the nose is high, a light seen over the nose gives the impression of excess altitude.

If all this sounds like we must have better than rudimentary instrument skill to take off safely at night, it's true. Only the instruments and the ability to use them dispel the illusions of the night sky. If you want to learn for yourself whether your instrument proficiency meets the demands of a VFR night takeoff, try an experiment. With a safety pilot and a hood aboard, climb to a safe altitude and establish the airplane in slow flight at lift-off speed. Then, put on the hood and fly a simple three-part maneuver on instruments.

1. Climb straight ahead for 1000 feet at best rate of climb speed.
2. Make a shallow-banked turn of 45 degrees.

3. Climb another 500 feet on the new heading and level off on a predetermined altitude.

If you are able to climb and turn within 5 knots of best rate of climb speed, maintain desired headings within 10 degrees, and level out within 100 feet of the objective altitude, you can feel confident with a VFR night departure. If, however, your instrument skill has rusted a bit, you might want to hone your hood work before making a night takeoff.

FACT 3. At night it is difficult to read the weather that lies ahead and around. During the day, experience has taught us how to interpret the weather ahead by what we see—cloud textures, hues in the sky, wind against the water and ground below. But at night, without the visual clues, we can fly right into where we should not enter.

We must add a nighttime flavor to our Flight Service Station (FSS) weather briefings. And we must obtain these nighttime briefings even for a local flight. Keep in mind the three factors that are common in night-flying accidents, accident report after accident report. First, the pilot is usually not instrument rated. Second, the weather is usually so-so for VFR daytime flight. Often, however, there are patches of light scattered precipitation in the area—the sort that we just fly through during the day. Third, the accident usually happens over a rural area devoid of ground lighting. So, examine the briefing for those things that are only minor daytime navigation annoyances but could produce a nighttime hazard.

Scattered Showers. Scattered precipitation is easy to avoid or even fly through during day (assuming the rain is light enough to see through). But at night you're into it before you see it coming. The same light spray of rain on the windscreen that is of little concern during day gives a smear of instant IFR at night.

High Ceilings. A 6000-foot broken or overcast ceiling during the day presents little difficulty to VFR flying. At night, however, that extent of cloud cover just hides too many of the stars that help over the dark areas. A sloping overcast seen above reflected city lights is particularly deceitful. With the horizon hidden in darkness, the pilot often tries to hold the wings parallel to the cloud base. This can quickly produce a premium-grade vertigo.

Low-level Scattered Clouds. Low scattered clouds present three major hazards to VFR night navigation. First, you can fly right into them without much warning—and someone else may be doing the same from the other side. Second, if you decide to stay beneath the clouds, most other pilots have too. You force yourself to fly in a narrow band of congested airspace. Third, if you decide to fly "on top," you run the high risk of getting *caught* on top, a very uncomfortable nighttime VFR situation. With the cooling temperatures of night, a scattered layer can quickly become broken or overcast. At night you often cannot see it occurring until it is too late for a safe letdown.

Reduced Visibility. Marginal visibility of 7 or 8 miles is not often critical to our daytime flying. It usually leaves enough landmarks open for navigation, lets us see the weather ahead, and provides adequate margin for further deterioration so that we can plan to be in a position to land if it drops to 5 or 6 miles.

Reduced visibility does not treat us so kindly at night, however. Reliable lighted landmarks are often separated by several miles. Also, any restriction to visibility further hampers our efforts to read the weather ahead. At night, deteriorating visibility is often difficult to discern. I have a pilot friend of several hundred flight hours who thoroughly enjoys night flying. She has some good words concerning visibility and VFR night flying.

> Prevailing visibility is a major concern to me when planning a night flight. I want at least 12 miles, coupled with a favorable forecast for the evening. This may seem too conservative to many, but I don't think so—I've done a *lot* of night flying. The 12 miles of visibility at takeoff reassures me that *should* visibility drop another 2 or 3 miles, I'm still OK.

And there's the fact that my plane is single engine. I maintain it carefully, but I do know it can quit. The prospect of a daytime off-airport landing doesn't frighten me. I know I can handle it. But the prospect of an off-airport landing at night is another matter. I realize full well that I'd probably get hurt. At night I want a runway within easy reach, one that I can *find*. Therefore, I want to see far enough that I have an airport beacon in sight 90 percent of the time. I want visibility that has the next beacon nearly in sight as the one behind fades from view. I often need to plan a crooked route to make this possible. But I feel the extra time en route is worth the insurance it gives. When the unexpected arrives, I want a *findable* runway close at hand. *Un*-beaconed airports just won't do — just *try* to locate that airport when the need to get the plane on the ground is critical.

Then there is the matter of spotting traffic in a timely manner. Navigation lights are not the easiest things to find, particularly at relatively low altitudes around city lights. Then once you spot them, it takes several glances to determine their altitude, range, and heading. Let's say I'm flying at night through only 8 miles visibility. If that traffic's cruising speed is just 50 percent greater than that of my own plane, we will close that 8 miles in 1 minute and 36 seconds. In that time I would need to first spot the traffic, then determine its altitude, distance, and course, then decide if it presented a hazard, then decide what I needed to do, then move the controls, then let the plane respond to the controls, and still leave enough time for my plane to move out of the way. There are just too many "thens." It could *take* 1 minute and 36 seconds for all of that to happen.

Then I must consider that even in my short flying career, I've encountered three planes running at night without lights. Did a pilot inadvertently switch them off, or did a fuse blow, or did the pilot just forget? Who knows? Fortunately in each case the sky was CAVU and their shapes were seen in the starlight as ghostly images. Would I have seen them through restricted visibility? Maybe.

I enjoy night flight. It's the only time my schedule lets me fly. But I *do* want at least 12 miles visibility before I take off.

Strong Winds Aloft. A brisk breeze at altitude rarely deters a straight course from A to B during the day. We just crank in the needed wind-correction angle, shift the terrain around a few degrees in our mind, and check off each landmark as it passes beneath. But things are not as easy at night. We can't see what the wind is doing to our ground track. The cockeyed view that the wind correction gives to the lighted landmarks can soon have us thinking that we're going the wrong way.

Then too, significant winds aloft (20 knots or so) are often accompanied by turbulence. The same daytime light or moderate turbulence that only reminds us that we're flying can adversely affect our performance at night. This would more likely happen to a pilot already geographically confused about position due to wind drift. Then, the bucking of even moderate turbulence could produce further confusion or even vertigo.

When deciding how much turbulence to accept for a night flight, we might gain some insight by examining the FAA's descriptions (adapted from Table 16.2 in *Aviation Weather Services*) of turbulence intensities.

Light turbulence. The pilot may expect light turbulence to produce slight, erratic changes in aircraft attitude and altitude. Inside the cockpit, passengers will feel slight strain against seat belts, and loose objects may move about.

Moderate turbulence. Moderate turbulence disturbs the plane's attitude and altitude to the extent that airspeed varies. The plane, however, remains in positive control. The passengers feel definite pulls against seat belts and objects may become dislodged.

Severe turbulence. Severe turbulence causes large, abrupt changes in attitude, altitude, and airspeed. There is momentary loss of aircraft control. Passengers are yanked against harness and belt, and loose objects are tossed about.

Extreme turbulence. Extreme turbulence throws the plane about violently. Control is impossible. Structural damage *is* possible. Passengers could be injured if not tightly harnessed.

As we compare the reported intensities to our willingness to accept them, keep in mind that the wind rarely blows constant. Light turbulence is normally punctuated by moderate. Moderate turbulence is usually punctuated with blasts of severe. Severe turbulence is invariably punctuated by torrents of extreme.

VFR Radar Advisories. Even if you do not avail yourself of radar services during the day, by all means take advantage of them at night. I know for a fact that we spot only one-third of our significant traffic. I know this because I keep score on myself, and I'm looking as hard as any pilot out there. When ATC advises me of significant traffic that I've not already spotted, that's a mark against me. If I've already seen it, that's a point in my favor. I only score one out of three.

To prevent the collision takes only one pilot to see. But even with both pilots working, that still leaves a 33 percent chance of things that go bump in the night. That's where VFR radar traffic advisories come in — ATC provides that needed third set of eyes. If your proposed night flight expects crowded skies and radar services are *not* available, the advisability of a takeoff is in question.

Night Takeoff Procedures

In general, night takeoff procedures vary little from those made in daytime. But there are *some* extra steps that should play into the action. Here are a dozen tips that you might find useful.

TIP 1. Explain the boarding procedure to the passengers. Let your flashlight point out foot spuds and handholds. Stand by to assist each passenger into the cockpit. If you fly a high-winged light plane, be sure to explain *how* old pilots got those creases in their heads — before you let the passengers even get *near* the trailing edge.

TIP 2. The same printer who publishes Bible verses on pinheads prints the radio frequencies on the sectional chart. Trying to find and read them at night just takes too much of your eyeball time away from spotting traffic. Therefore, research the chart and the *Airport/Facility Directory* before the flight and reduce all anticipated frequencies to a simple radio frequency log (Fig. 5.4).

TIP 3. I always carry two flashlights. I prefer the disposable pencil-type. Each is good for a half-hour of reliable light and is easy to hold in the side of your mouth cigar-fashion, leaving your hands free. Also, their pinpoint of light does not blind your night vision.

TIP 4. Fuses do blow and breakers do trip. Finding a replacement fuse and replacing it during the day presents no problem. Doing the same at night in a darkened cockpit *can* be a problem unless you've had recent experience. Therefore, let a part of your preflight inspection include a dress rehearsal. Find where the spare fuses are stored, determine how to select the right amperage, and go through the replacement procedure. Take time to locate the

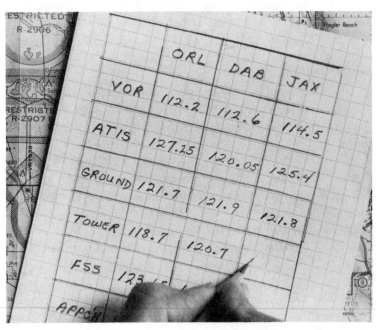

5.4. *Prepare a simple radio log before the flight.*

circuit breakers; some manufacturers hide them in the most gosh-awful places.

TIP 5. Use a bright green marking pen to lay out your course on the sectional chart. (The charts are predominately red and blue.) Use the pen to circle useful lighted landmarks about every 20 miles and note the expected lapsed time from takeoff to each. Then you will know that what you *do* see is what you *should* see. Dead-reckoning navigation is important to night flight since most landmarks are hidden in darkness. Become an expert with your flight computer.

TIP 6. Clean the *inside* of the windscreen as well as the exterior before a night flight. The inside film that goes unnoticed by day restricts vision at night.

TIP 7. When cranking at night, you can whack someone unless you give a warning. Simply shouting, Clear! won't do the job. Pedestrians can't tell which plane the yell comes from when walking a dark ramp. So turn on the navigation lights a moment before you "clear." Since these small lights place only a minimum drain against the battery, you can keep them on right through the starting procedure.

TIP 8. Don't taxi without the landing or taxi light on—any more than you would drive a car at night without lights—no matter how slowly you are driving. Taxi very slowly at night. A landing light's cone is focused close to the airplane and you can easily out-taxi your light's range.

Don't taxi too close to the plane ahead. Planes don't have brake lights and it takes a moment to tell that the plane ahead has stopped.

TIP 9. Refer to your airspeed indicator to determine the time to rotate. A nighttime takeoff run gives the illusion of excess speed and the time needed to gain rotate speed seems to drag by.

TIP 10. Know, from daytime experience, the pitch displayed on the
        attitude indicator during a climb at best rate of climb speed.
Don't depend solely on this instrument, however. Just integrate it
with your use of the outside visual references.

TIP 11. Keep your runway heading in mind as a standard reference
        for course guidance during your initial climbout. Relate it to
your heading indicator.

Use your heading indicator to establish a wind-correction
angle if there is a crosswind. Significant wind drift can occur and it
is difficult to detect at night. To estimate the correction needed,
apply a rule of thumb from an earlier chapter: for typical light-
plane climb speeds (65 to 95 knots), apply 1 degree of wind-correction angle for each 1 knot of crosswind component. Thus, if you
have a 10-knot crosswind component from the right, steer 10 degrees to the right of the runway heading. While not a perfect correction, it will do the job for that critical first thousand feet of
initial climbout.

TIP 12. Learn to use and trust your instruments during the takeoff
        sequence. You need not be instrument rated to do so — as long
as there are adequate outside visual references and as long as you
only *integrate* instrument indications *with* outside references. But
don't think for a minute that you can control your aircraft solely
by instruments. You can't, unless you are really instrument quali-
fied. (Several years ago the FAA ran an experiment. They picked
twenty-four non-instrument-rated pilots, flew them into actual
IFR, and then gave them the controls in straight and level cruise
flight. Not one pilot maintained control for a significant time.
Would you like to know the average time before they lost control?
Twenty-two seconds.)

When you take off at night, *integrate* the instruments to *verify*
what you already see outside. Let the attitude indicator confirm
that your wings are level during that climbout. Verify your continued climb performance with the VSI, tachometer, airspeed indica-

tor, and altimeter. Let the heading indicator assist you with a course that is true.

So, there we have some basic considerations to keep in mind as we plan and fly our night departure. Put them to use and you will make one satisfying night takeoff after another. Take the plane to the night sky. I know that you will like the pilot you meet — and that you will enjoy the pleasure of your own company.

IN REVIEW: Night Takeoffs

PREFLIGHT REMINDERS

- Any reduction of oxygen in our blood, or any toxic substance, seriously affects night vision.
- At night, distance seems compressed and even minutes seem drawn out.
- We must have better than rudimentary instrument skill to take off safely at night.
- We must add a nighttime flavor to the FSS weather briefing.
- Three common factors that run through night-flying accident reports are a non-instrument-rated pilot, minor weather factors that are of little daytime concern, rural areas devoid of ground lighting.
- At night a light shower can put a smear of instant IFR on the windscreen.
- Even high ceilings at night can hide too much starlight.
- Low-level scattered clouds can quickly close to a ceiling at night.
- Reduced visibility is far more critical to night flight than to day-time navigation.
- Wind drift is difficult to discern at night.
- Even if you do not avail yourself of radar services during the day, use them at night.
- At night, stand by to assist each passenger aboard.

- Research the sectional chart and *Airport/Facility Directory* before the flight and reduce all anticipated radio frequencies to a simple radio frequency log.
- Always carry a flashlight.
- Know where the spare fuses are located and practice installing them.
- Use a bright marking pen to lay out your course on the sectional chart.
- Clean the inside of the windscreen as well as the exterior before a night flight.
- Turn on the navigation lights before you crank the engine.
- During initial climbout, keep the runway heading in mind for course guidance.
- Learn to integrate instrument indications with outside references; don't depend on instruments alone unless you are IFR rated.

IN-FLIGHT AIDS

RADIO FREQUENCY LOG

STATIONS

FACILITY					
VOR					
ATIS					
GROUND CONTROL					
TOWER					
FSS					
DEPARTURE APPROACH					
ATC CENTER					
UNICOM					
FLIGHT WATCH					
EMERGENCY					

5.5. Prepare a simple radio-frequency log before you depart.

I have lifted my plane from the Nairobi airport for perhaps a thousand flights and I have never felt her wheels glide from the earth into the air without knowing the uncertainty and the exhilaration of firstborn adventure.

—**Beryl Markham**
West with the Night

CHAPTER SIX

Tailwheel Takeoffs

F orgive my dated concept: Piper's little yellow J-3 Cub is still my favorite. When a Cub's engine fires, you can feel the plane come to life by just touching fingers to the trembling, taut fabric that surrounds. There is something about the ship's gently rocking taxi that promises adventure, romance. And leaning back against that tailwheel changes a takeoff from *flying* to *barnstorming*. Even the folks left behind find the *ta-pok-a-ta, ta-pok-a-ta* of a Cub climbing from a grass strip a friendly sound. Aloft, I can leave that clam-shell door open, stick my face out and have it flattened by prop blast, or contemplate the unplexiglassed countryside drifting below. The whispered return to Earth behind a throttled 65 lets play the wind-in-the-wires song of flight. Those donut tires practically guarantee are-we-down-yet landings, and I do enjoy reaching up to grab those bars to hoist out of the seat. Over 50 years the ship's been around. I can't believe it even as I write it – 50 years. I've flown most and still the Cub remains so close; I can't figure it out – for the life of me, I can't figure it out.

Tailwheel Departures – the Facts

First of all, tailwheel takeoffs are fun. You need to try them if you have not already done so. You will need an instructor aboard until you get the hang of them; don't try it alone or you may rack up a perfectly innocent airplane. They are not difficult, just different. But you should understand some of the differences even before you climb aboard.

The first thing that you will notice (if by luck you are short enough) is that you cannot see straight ahead. The low tailwheel and the high-pointing cowl prevent that. So when you taxi, don't do it in a straight line. Instead, S-turn: turn left, stretch neck right; turn right, stretch neck left. If you meet a modern tricycle-gear airplane coming your way, don't expect the pilot to recognize your plight. Simply pull over to the side and stop to let those stream-lined wings, sleek-swept tail, and purring engine scoot past.

Into your taxi, you will soon discover that wind plays an important part in driving a tailwheeler along the ground. When taxi-ing a tricycled airplane, a normal breeze passes almost unnoticed. The nosewheel acts as a sea anchor against the puff of wind that hits the vertical stabilizer. Directional control remains positive. But in that same gentle breeze a tailwheeler tries to weather-vane like a wind sock. The vertical tail becomes a perfect vane, and the position of the main wheels (*ahead* of the center of gravity, rather than *behind* as in a nosewheeler) provides an excellent pivot point (Fig 6.1).

The answer here lies in a constant awareness of the wind's direction as you taxi. Plan ahead. If an upcoming turn will force the wind against your vertical stabilizer, decide which way it will try to weather-vane you in the turn. Then slow down and decide whether or not the wind's direction or force calls for more or for less turning on your part. If the wind is against your turn, only firm rudder action will pull you through it (Fig. 6.2). If on the other hand, the wind's direction will try to swing you through the turn, then you had better stay pretty light on your toes as you enter that turn—and be ready to catch *oversteering* (Fig. 6.3). When taxiing straight ahead, deflect the controls so that the wind cannot catch up under them. For example, a trailing wind is best handled with the elevator deflected downward.

There's going to be an extra step in the takeoff run. It happens

6.1. Centers of gravity are located with purpose. If a tailwheeler's center of gravity was ahead of the gear, the plane would rest with its nose to the ground. An aft center of gravity would have the nosewheeler's tail on the ground.

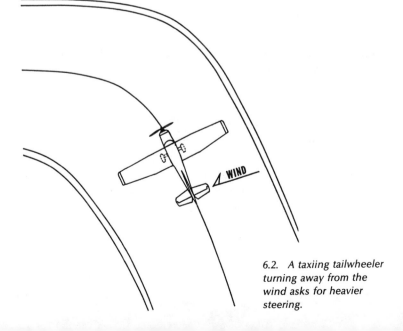

6.2. A taxiing tailwheeler turning away from the wind asks for heavier steering.

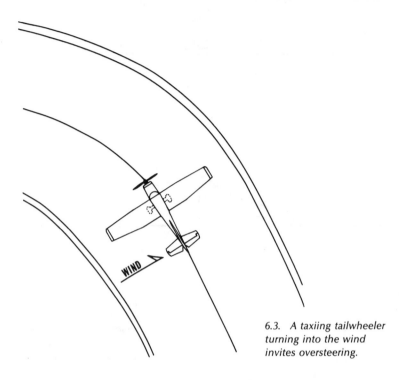

6.3. A taxiing tailwheeler turning into the wind invites oversteering.

when you lift the tail level prior to lift-off. You will recall that a tricycle's takeoff run had two moments of left-turning tendency that needed rudder correction. The first occurred in the initial seconds of the run—slipstream effect. The second occurred at the point of lift-off—P factor. A tailwheeler's takeoff run, however, includes a *third* moment of left-turning tendency—when you lift the tail level prior to lift-off. *Gyroscopic precession* is the culprit. The spinning propeller arc acts like a gyroscope, which tries to remain stable. When a force is applied to one side of its arc, it counters with a force 90 degrees from its axis and directly opposite its direction of turn. When we lift the tail we create pressure on the spinning gyroscopic propeller arc. Since the arc is spinning to the right, a left-turning force is created. You need to be ready with a nudge of right rudder to prevent a swerve.

There is another source of swerve whenever the tailwheel aircraft is rolling — *adverse yaw*. Again, you will recall from an earlier chapter that erroneously trying to correct a swerve with ailerons produces *opposite steering*. That is, if you attempt to straighten a *left* swerve with *right* aileron instead of rudder, the swerve intensifies. Well, in a tailwheeler this adverse yaw also intensifies. The position of a tailwheeler's center of gravity relative to the main gear adds a pendulum effect to any swerve — it tries to gain momentum.

To understand why this happens, picture two planes rolling along — one a tricycle, the other a tailwheeler. Which is more prone to swerve? The tailwheeler, naturally. Its center of gravity *behind* the main wheels practically invites a turn end-around. The nosewheeler's center of gravity *ahead* of the wheels, on the other hand, helps the plane roll straight ahead.

Once a swerve starts, in which plane is that swerve more apt to grow? Again, the tailwheeler. Its rearward center of gravity acts like a pendulum. The nosewheel of the tricycled plane, on the other hand, acts like a brace against the swerve. The secret here, if there is a secret, is to anticipate the tailwheeler's next move. Don't allow the inevitable small swerve to intensify. Anticipate the swerve so that small rudder corrections are given the instant they are needed. This *feel* to anticipate is not difficult to learn. Just liken it to a couple of childhood games. Do you remember, as a kid, balancing on a rail while standing with one foot behind the other? You soon learned to feel which way to tip your body English to prevent a spill. Where did you feel your balance? In your seat. Remember the "slow" race on your bicycle — who could ride the slowest without falling? Again, the seat of your pants told you which way to weave the handlebar. The same goes with anticipating those inevitable small swerves in a tailwheel airplane — concentration and the seat of your pants.

So, with the background information in mind find an available tailwheeler and a willing instructor, dust off the seat of your pants, climb aboard, and do give tailwheel airplanes a try. I think you are going to like the experience.

And Some Fun

Hey, instead of renting a taildragger, why don't you think about buying one? Aw, come on now — fun is what flying's all about, and I only said *think* about it. Its cost and upkeep wouldn't be much more than buying a new car on time. Just keep the old jalopy and buy a set of wings. Even pull in a partner if you want. Here are half-dozen seasoned veterans to choose from.

CESSNA 140. Cessna started building the model 140 (Fig. 6.4) soon after World War II. This tailwheeler is a natural for any pilot trained in 150s or 152s. They all fly about the same. There are a bunch of them still around and you should be able to pick up a nice one for about $9,000.

6.4. **Cessna 140** *(Seats 2)*
Engine: 85 HP
Cruise speed: 85 knots
Range: 440 nautical
Useful load: 650 pounds
Landing speed: 36 knots
(Photo courtesy of Cessna Aircraft Company)

CESSNA 180. The Cessna 180 (Fig. 6.5) is a real workhorse and about the easiest plane to fly that I've ever known. Not even a hint of bad habits. Take out the back seats and you have a real load hauler, over a half-ton of useful load. Why, you and a buddy could make a fortune carrying watermelons up to the oilriggers on the North Slope. Bet they'd pay fifty bucks apiece for them just to see how far they could spit the seeds. Plan on paying around $28,000 for one in good shape.

6.5. **Cessna 180** (Seats 4)
Engine: 230 HP
Cruise speed: 140 knots
Range: 550 nautical
Useful load: 1160 pounds
Landing speed: 50 knots
(Photo courtesy of Cessna Aircraft Company)

PIPER J-3 CUB. The J-3 (Fig. 6.6) takes you back to the basics; even the fuel is gauged by cork and wire. The cramped cockpit that reeks of hot engine oil hands you a long wooden stick with which to guide the controls and lets you hold that clattering engine in your lap. There are a lot of J-3s scattered about at grass fields to give you a wide selection. Owners, however, are reluctant to part

6.6.   **Piper J-3** *(Seats 2 in tandem)*
       Engine: You only need half of what it has.
       Cruise speed: The cars below do pass.
       Range: The next grass strip.
       Useful load: Anything you can cram in.
       Landing speed: Dog trot.
       (Photo by John Tate)

with them. But drive a hard bargain filled with promises of tender loving care and someone may favor you with a little jewel for $10,000 or so.

PIPER SUPER CUB. If you like the J-3 but think it a bit puny, spring for a Super Cub (Fig. 6.7). While a J-3 can get out of a football field, the Super Cub can do nearly the same from a tennis court. It's a tough old bird with rugged gear and really doesn't need a runway as such; any good fishing spot with a decent run of beach is fair game. When time comes to haul your catch home, the Super Cub can carry about any load you can manage to stuff aboard. Lots of them are around for maybe twice the price of a J-3.

MAULE. If you're looking for a modern reproduction of an old-fashioned airplane, the Maule (Fig. 6.8) might be your ship. Fabric covered, but fiberglassed; tailwheeled, but with the *easy*

6.7. **Piper Super Cub** *(Seats 2 in tandem)*
Engine: 150 HP
Cruise speed: 100 knots
Range: 400 nautical
Useful load: 680 pounds
Landing speed: 38 knots
(Photo courtesy of Piper Aircraft Corporation)

6.8. **Maule M-4** *(Seats 4)*
Engine: 145 HP
Cruise speed: 135 knots
Range: 650 nautical
Useful load: 980 pounds
Landing speed: 39 knots
(Photo courtesy of Maule Aircraft Company)

Maule patented tailwheel. Spacious too, it holds four with lots of leg and shoulder room. And it gets you there in a hurry; even the early models with the 145 Continental deliver a mile an hour for each horsepower. Somewhere around $10,000 should do just fine.

TAYLORCRAFT. Gilbert Taylor was the guy who designed the Cub for William Piper. Later, when Taylor set up his own plant, he took the design ideas of the Cub, streamlined them a bit, and put the seats side by side for a comfortable fit (if the two of you are small and quite good friends).

The Taylorcraft (Fig. 6.9) is considered a desirable antique. Yet it is very easy to fly and gets you there in reasonable time, and parts and engines are easy to come by. If you are on a tight budget, this might be the one for you. About $8,000.

6.9. **Taylorcraft BC12** *(Seats 2)*
Engine: 65 HP
Cruise speed: 85 knots
Range: 290 miles
Useful load: 450 pounds
Landing speed: 35 knots
(Photo courtesy of Experimental Aircraft Association, Inc.)

So, think about buying a tailwheeler of your own. If you *do* buy one, do me a favor. Some spring, gas it up and fly it down to the Experimental Aircraft Association's Sun 'n Fun Fly-in, which is held in Lakeland, Florida, the second week of each April. After you tie down, holler my name with full lung-power. I'll trot right over and we'll talk airplane stuff.

IN REVIEW: Tailwheel Takeoffs

- S-turn when taxiing a tailwheel airplane.
- When taxiing, plan ahead to anticipate the wind's force against the vertical fin in an upcoming turn.
- Gyroscopic precession tends to slew a tailwheeler left as the tail is raised during the takeoff run.
- The effects of adverse yaw are intensified in a tailwheel airplane.

IN-FLIGHT AIDS

AIRCRAFT DATA

1. Rotate speed:_____
2. Best angle of climb speed: _____
3. Best rate of climb speed: _____
4. Stalling speed (takeoff configuration): _____
5. Fuel endurance: _____
6. Climb power: _____
7. Cruise power: _____
8. Weight and balance verified? _____
9. Takeoff distance required: _____
10. Recommended flaps: _____
11. Abort/stop distance: _____

6.10. As with any unfamiliar aircraft, research the plane's manual before you fly.

CHAPTER SEVEN

Cardinal Rules for Perfect Takeoffs

Well, you've just had six chapters full of words on how to launch an airplane. But these days we seem to like our information in capsule form. So, with this in mind, I'd like to list ten rules that I think are of cardinal importance to safe and satisfactory takeoffs.

1

Never take a defective plane to the air. This sounds simplistic, I know. But it happens very often and with great regularity. All too often the witnesses say something akin to, "We could hear the engine misfiring at the start of the roll." A thorough preflight that follows an adequate checklist is a pilot's first line of defense. A good preflight inspection depends on a pilot's concentration, methodology, and attitude. When conducting the inspection, a pilot should focus *all* attention on the aircraft. Conversation with passengers, worrying about upcoming navigation, or any other distraction robs the preflight's efficiency.

An aircraft inspection must be methodical. If you find yourself missing a checklist item or checking the list out of sequence, you must take heed that your mind is wandering. You should stop the preflight at that point and start again at the top of the written checklist.

A pilot's attitude toward the preflight inspection is critical. All too often pilots conduct a preflight with the preconceived notion that the plane is probably OK. The pilot who begins preflighting only 10 minutes before departure time is a good example of this. That pilot obviously does not *expect* to find anything wrong that requires repair or service. And since that pilot *expects* to find nothing, discrepancies are bound to slip past.

Be highly suspicious of your aircraft. Let stubbornness work you through the checklist to ferret out any hidden hazards.

2

Evaluate the overall takeoff situation at hand and relate it to the plane's takeoff performance chart. It is so easy, as we prepare for takeoff, to say to ourselves, That is an approved runway before me; I am flying an approved airplane; therefore, everything will work out OK. To say this is to say that we are willing to rely on past successes. Every takeoff, however, must stand on its own. Even that runway that has accepted your plane so many times in the past may refuse to do so today. For you are now attempting to take off with today's crosswind component, today's weight and balance, today's density altitude, today's unique set of takeoff variables.

Remember, as you use your charts, that they must relate to the *real world* that you face on takeoff. Be ready to modify the charts' values to meet the *un*charted values that challenge the takeoff — for example, the higher-than-50-foot obstacle, the softer-than-contemplated surface, the wind that blows slightly from the tail — all the variables of the real world.

3

Adhere to the manufacturer's takeoff recommendations. The manufacturer *knows* what is best for its airplane. There is a fallacy directed toward many aircraft that says, This is a forgiving airplane. But in reality this is true of *no* airplane. All planes have operating limits. In light planes, especially, the parameters of these limits are quite narrow in terms of speed, loading, balance, power, and aerodynamic force. Operate the plane within these limits and it will perform as expected. Operate *beyond* these limits, however, and you are breaking new ground. Manufacturers state their tried and proven procedures with the express motive of keeping pilots within the design limits of operation.

The need to keep a plane within its design limits is reflected in the basic truth of flying, which simply says

> Plane and sky accept no excuses and grant no special consider-
> ations. It makes no difference whether we walk the Earth as
> good or bad, wise or foolish, poor or rich. When we enter the
> cockpit, we leave behind our Earthbound differences. We touch
> the controls as one—a pilot. If our actions are *right,* the flight
> will probably succeed. If our actions are *not* right, the flight may
> likely fail.

4

Know what you and your plane, as a team, can deliver. Once you know the airplane's capabilities through a study of performance charts and recommended procedures, you have half the equation in hand. The other half rests in the knowledge of your own abilities to match the aircraft's performance. Questions arise that need answers. How much crosswind can I handle? If obstacle clearance is critical, can I pin down best-angle climb speed and hold it there? How much tailwind can I accept? There is an old bromide that goes, If I really get in a jam, I will be able to act beyond my normal ability. But it has been my observation that the reverse is true: when truly behind the eight ball, pilots usually act far *below* their normal capabilities. When facing a critical takeoff, then, it is important to know, through demonstrated actions, your own limitations and not depend on a skill that just isn't there.

Now, I am not saying that you should never reach beyond your acquired skill. You should. It is the only way to increase your skill. There is a definite truth concerning pilot skill: it will either grow or erode, but it will never remain unchanged.

So at times, go beyond yourself. But do so at times of your own choosing, in a controlled situation, and with a safety net. This best safety net is having a good instructor on board. With this in mind, I offer a recommendation to any pilot who flies the infrequent schedule that recreational flying usually imposes. I recommend a bimonthly, dual, recurrent-training flight. Remain a student of the art. Select maneuvers that reflect your primary flight concerns. And by all means, let your workouts include crosswind takeoffs and landings, the major producers of flying accidents.

5

Plan an abort point before the takeoff gets under way. Don't leave this important decision until the moment to employ it is at hand. If you do not already hold the commitment to abort if necessary, you may be subconsciously committed to "press on regardless" when things start to go wrong.

I am convinced that had pilots executed a timely abort, 90 percent of the takeoff accidents would have never happened. Accordingly, I advise my students: When planning a takeoff, hold in mind your *primary* plan to abort. Then, if you reach your abort point and everything is still OK, put your *secondary* plan into action — complete the takeoff.

6

Plan an adequate safety margin of runway length. The unforeseen can creep into any takeoff — a headwind that decides to die, a cockpit distraction that costs aircraft control and runway length, a simple misreading of a performance chart. As a rule of thumb, I like a runway that exceeds 150 percent of the calculated minimum distance required.

7

Have in mind an emergency landing area. The worst time for
an emergency landing to come your way is during those first
thousand feet of altitude following takeoff. So before a departure
from your home airport, know where relative safety lies. And
when in the landing pattern at an unfamiliar airport, scout out a
likely area that gives a measure of safety to your departure that will
soon ensue.

8

Keep your eyes on the road during taxi and the takeoff run.
Should you look down within the cockpit while moving — to
set frequencies, for example, or to reach for the charts lying in the
back seat — you run the risk of hitting something or, at the very
least, swerving. Imagine the impact that a healthy swerve on the
takeoff run has on a passenger, even if no damage occurs. Picture
the passenger's perception — the sight of the runway gone askew,
the sound of squalling tires, the feel of a swinging tail. It's enough
to make the hardiest passenger opt for Greyhound on the return
trip, and the pilot has thereby hurt aviation.

9

Make every takeoff a practice takeoff. It is easy to do. As you
prepare for takeoff, meticulously adhere to your written
checklists. During taxi, keep yourself *exactly* astride the taxiway's
center line. Plan ahead to maintain a constant taxi speed devoid of
any need for corrective braking or blasts of throttle. Make the
takeoff run with the nosewheel constantly holding the center
stripes. Rotate at the precise instant and hit best rate of climb right
on the mark. Absolutely kill wind drift with headings that you
deliberately choose and hold, and level off precisely on your desired cruising altitude.

Not only is this practice *easy* with every takeoff, it is also *vital* to improving your skills. The accuracy and finesse that you develop through constant practice with each *normal* takeoff gives you a reserve of competence that may be needed to face the *abnormal* departure. Look at it this way. Imagine that you are riding in the rear seat during two separate takeoffs. Each pilot has a different attitude toward departures. The one strives for perfection with every takeoff—smooth control with everything right down the center lines, hitting each and every speed on the mark. The other pilot is satisfied just to pour on the coal and get the plane off the ground before anything bad happens. Now, let's ride with each of those pilots while preparing to make a maximum-gross-weight takeoff from a narrow, short runway with 15-knot gusts blowing across it—at night. Which pilot has better prospects for a safe departure? Which pilot has the needed reserve of competence? Which pilot would you prefer to sit behind? The constant quest for perfection with each and every normal takeoff, then, develops and stores skill and knowledge, your own reserve of competence.

10

Exert a 100 percent effort with each takeoff. Perfect takeoffs don't just happen. You *make* them happen. This 100 percent effort begins long before you have the throttle in hand. As you research the conditions, evaluate your own skill and be sure your plane is up to the task. A maximum effort here means that you *know* the factors that influence takeoffs, that you have *learned* your plane's capabilities, and that you have *developed* your skill to control that capability. With each departure you, in fact, have a total awareness of the environment, the airplane, and yourself. Make a commitment to that degree of effort and you will not fail to deliver perfect takeoff after perfect takeoff.

Epilogue

Flying is like a wiener roast—to have purpose that is enjoyed, it must be shared. Take your plane to the dawn-lit sky and race the unrisen beam to that small pink cloud floating there by the morning star. Reach altitude by that moment the fresh-slanting sun first lights the shaded glens below with powdered gold. Set a course toward your secret sharer. Aim your plane toward that small town ahead and below that beckons with its silver water tower. That silver tower guarantees the presence of the dreamer below—a young dreamer of planes and skies, back pressed flat against crushed grass, who has tracked your plane since it first droned over the western horizon.

Even now, as you slide overhead, that dreamer is wondering—wondering if the sun's flash against the wings disturbs the pilot within, wondering what it sounds like and what it feels like to be in the cockpit, wondering if the chance to know will ever happen. You must do your part. You must make your wings and engine *speak* to that dreamer below. Your flying must speak to that young person of the things a dreamer-turned-doer may expect to learn within a cockpit. It is not enough that you fly with skill. To have significance, your flying must accomplish something as well.

Make contact! Waggle your wings. Then point your plane along a section line and get ready for a pair of back-to-back steep 720-degree power turns. Now roll into the natural grace of a near-vertical, 60-degree banked turn to port. Pin the nose against the rotating horizon and feed in power against the pull of two g's, twice around and then roll to starboard for two more sweeps.

Keep your turns perfect. Don't spoil the song of harmonious cylinders with a skid that shoves the prop sidewise to the wind, to say *Brraaap!* for all the sky to hear. Don't allow a faulty rate of roll to bend the symmetry of a precision turn. Fly your turns with a perfection that lets your engine and wings say to that dreamer below,

> *This is flying at its best, and one day you too will learn of the freedoms that lie within a perfectly flown chandelle, or a lazy eight, or a pair of steep power turns. But until that day, keep trusting the dictates of your own intellect. Listen to those who have traveled before you — yes, but not too rigidly. For whether they are fifty or sixty or seventy-five, none has yet gained one-tenth of what you dream of achieving before the decade is out. And if your logic tells you that what is commonly called right is wrong, hold faith with your own reason. Let your life accept the pleasures of your* own *intellect — and the responsibilities for your* own *mistakes. Use each win, each loss, as a stepping-stone toward your own total awareness. And in that regard, your living will be a lot like flying.*

Level your wings from the turns and dip a tip farewell. Bank back to the west, set your course, ease the power down a smidge, and slide the sky homeward. Turn into the pattern and throttle back for the landing. Touch down and roll to a stop, satisfied with a flight well flown, for to fly with skill is not enough. To have significance, our flying must also have purpose.

My very best goes with you.

Yours sincerely,

Ron Fowler

Christmas, Florida
Autumn 1991

APPENDIX

Some Rules of Thumb Concerning Takeoffs

- **Minimum takeoff fuel quantity**
  Do not take off with less than a quarter-tank showing on the gauges.

- **Prolonged cranking**
  If prolonged cranking becomes necessary, allow the starter 1 minute of cooling between each 20-second interval of cranking.

- **Engine leaning**
  To insure optimum performance and a predictable fuel endurance, lean the engine any time it is producing no more than 75 percent of power.

- **Crosswind limit of operation**
  Do not attempt a takeoff when the crosswind component exceeds one-third of the plane's stall speed.

- **Calculating crosswind component**
  1. If the wind lies within 30 degrees of runway alignment, estimate the crosswind component at one-half the wind's velocity.
  2. If the wind lies from 30 to 60 degrees across the runway,

estimate the crosswind component at three-fourths the wind's velocity.

3. If the wind lies from 60 to 90 degrees across the runway, estimate the component at full wind velocity.

- **Runway surface conditions**
  1. If the grass runway is well mowed and dry, add 20 percent to the paved-runway "obstacle clearance distance."
  2. If the grass runway needs mowing or if the grass is wet, make that fudge factor 30 percent.
  3. If there is standing water on an unpaved strip, treat the take-off with a soft-field technique.

- **Estimating true airspeed**
  To estimate true airspeed, add 2 percent to indicated airspeed for each 1000 feet above sea level.

- **Converting a crosswind to its headwind component**
  If the sock is swinging within 30 degrees of runway alignment, consider it a direct headwind. Allow half the wind's velocity as a headwind component when the sock swings 30 to 60 degrees off the runway. And when the sock's angle with the runway exceeds 60 degrees, count the headwind zero.

- **Lightly loaded takeoffs**
  If the takeoff chart shows performance at maximum gross weight only, reduce the distance required by 5 percent for each 100 pounds below maximum allowable.

- **When to calculate weight and balance**
  Run a weight and balance calculation any time the seating capacity is over half-filled or when there is any luggage in the baggage compartment.

- **Minimum safe runway distance**
  Do not begin a takeoff unless the runway length provides 150

percent of the charted total-distance-to-clear-obstacle value for the prevailing conditions.

- **Abort/stop distance**
  If your runway has a safe 150 percent of the required total distance, then its midpoint provides a safe abort/stop distance.

- **Estimating jet-blast separation**

	Idle Power	Breakaway Power	Takeoff Power
Corporate-size jet	100 feet	200 feet	400 feet
Midsize jet	200 feet	400 feet	800 feet
Heavy jet	400 feet	800 feet	1600 feet

- **Estimating tailwind-takeoff distance**
  For each 5 knots of tailwind component, add 20 percent to the total distance required. (Include the usual 50 percent margin of safety when calculating the chart's total-distance value.)

- **Mountain turbulence**
  If stations near the mountains are reporting winds aloft in excess of 30 knots at mountaintop altitudes, postpone your flight.

- **Engine failure following takeoff**
  (Adapt the rules of thumb to accommodate your plane as suggested in Chapter 4.)
  1. If the engine fails below 500 AGL, select the best area within 30 degrees of turn and a _____ (distance) glide.
  2. If the engine fails between 500 and 1000 AGL, select a field that lies within 90 degree of turn and a _____ (distance) glide.
  3. If the engine fails above 1000 AGL and the airport boundary lies within _____ (distance), execute a turn and return to the field.

- **Estimating wind-correction angle during initial climbout**
  At typical light-plane climb speeds, apply 1 degree of wind-correction angle for each 1 knot of crosswind component.

Suggested Reading

I have noticed a common thread running through the lives of those pilots who excel at the controls. Most hold an awareness of aviation's roots and traditions. With this in mind I offer a short list of reading that you might enjoy. For the pilot with a keen interest in the evolvement of flying, the titles are listed in order of the story's unfolding.

Some of these books are now out of print. You must resort to secondhand bookstores and libraries. Even then you may be confronted with books falling apart with brittle, browning pages soon ready for discard. This is a shame, for these books are of the basic values that make airmanship. A hundred years from now pilots will fly equipment that we cannot even imagine today. Yet the values will remain unchanged. What these books have to say today will be important then. For this reason, I have a request: That those publishers who have not already done so reissue a printing on long-lasting acid-free paper.

The First to Fly, Sherwood Harris, New York: Simon and Schuster, 1970.

Goshawk Squadron, Derek Robinson, New York: The Viking Press, 1975.

The Courtney Entry, John Harris, New York: Doubleday and Co., Inc., 1969.

The Spirit of St. Louis, Charles A. Lindbergh, New York: Charles Scribner's Sons, 1953.

Wind, Sand and Stars, Antoine de Saint-Exupery, New York: Harcourt Brace Jovanovich, 1939.

Listen! the Wind, Anne Morrow Lindbergh, New York: Harcourt Brace Jovanovich, 1938.

West with the Night, Beryl Markham, San Francisco: North Point Press, 1983.

Last of the Bush Pilots, Harmon Helmericks, New York: Alfred A. Knopf, 1969.

Fate is the Hunter, Ernest K. Gann, New York: Simon and Schuster, 1961.

Signed with Their Honour, James Aldridge, Boston: Little, Brown and Co., 1942.

Pastoral, Nevil Shute, New York: William Morrow and Co., Inc., 1944.

A Gift of Wings, Richard Bach, New York: Delacorte Press, 1974.

Index

Aborted takeoff
  cardinal rule, 125
  fail-safe measure, 66–67
Acceleration
  aircraft loading, 62
  to cruise speed, 36
  deflected control surfaces, 25, 65
  and jet blast, 82
  short-field, 65
  soft-field, 73
Adverse yaw (aileron drag)
  crosswind correction, 28–29
  tailwheel airplane, 115
  on takeoff run, 27–28
Aileron drag. *See* Adverse yaw
Aircraft
  Cessna 140, 116
  Cessna 180, 117
  Maule, 118–20
  Piper Cherokee, 16
  Piper J-3 Cub, 111, 117–18
  Piper Super Cub, 118
  Taylorcraft, 120
Aircraft balance, 63–64
Aircraft loading
  boarding passengers, 103
  and climb performance, 62
  and ground run, 62
  lightening load, 54
  when to calculate, 64
Aircraft performance
  aircraft loading, 62
  field elevation, 56
  mountain airports, 84
  runway surface, 47–48
  runway temperature, 58–59
Airport/Facility Directory, 84
Airspeed control

during initial climb, 33
  at lift-off, 30–31
  at night, 105
  takeoff distance, 30–31
Airspeed indicator
  at night, 105
  preflight check, 16
  true airspeed, 57
Airspeeds
  best angle of climb, 52–54, 57
  best rate of climb, 33, 54, 106
  cruise, 36, 37
  rotate, 31, 52, 57, 74, 75, 105
  stall speed, 33, 52–54, 74, 89
  true airspeed, 57
Altimeter
  at night, 97, 107
  preflight check, 17
Ammeter
  in-flight discrepancy, 18
  preflight check, 11, 18
Attitude indicator
  at night, 96, 106
  preflight check, 16
Auxiliary fuel pump
  low-altitude use, 21
  preflight check, 10
  starting engine, 10
Avionics
  at engine start, 7
  preflight check, 23

Backside of power curve. *See* Region
  of reverse command
Best angle of climb speed
  mountain airports, 57
  and retracting flaps, 52

Best angle of climb speed (*cont.*)
  short-field operations, 52–54
  versus stall speed, 54
Best rate of climb speed
  establishing at night, 106
  during initial climb, 33
  practice, 126
  short-field operations, 54–56
Brakes
  in run-up area, 16
  seat position, 5
  starting engine, 10
  during takeoff run, 26
  taxiing, 13

Carburetor heat
  overrich mixture, 6
  preflight check, 22
Centerline stripes
  directional control, 27
  during initial climb, 33
  taking the runway, 24
Center of gravity
  effect on adverse yaw, 115
  taxiing tailwheelers, 112
Checklists
  climb, 43
  cruise, 43
  pretakeoff, 14–23, 42
  researching unfamiliar aircraft, 121
  starting engine 4–11, 41
  use of, 4, 12, 15, 122
Climbing
  and aircraft loading, 62
  checklist, 43
  cowl flaps, 6
  to cruise altitude, 35–36
  at high altitude, 56, 83
  initial climb, 32–34
Control surfaces
  aileron drag, 28–29, 115
  preflight check, 19
  takeoff run, 25
  taxiing, 13, 112
Cowl flaps, 6

Cranking, prolonged, 8, 10
Crosswind component
  estimating, 29
  maximum acceptable, 29
  mountain airports, 83, 85
Crosswind correction. *See also* Wind
  drift
  aileron drag, 28
  during initial climb, 33
  at lift-off, 31
  recurrent training, 125
  takeoff run, 28–29
  taxiing, 13

Defueling, 54
Directional control
  initial climb, 33
  at lift-off, 31–32
  runway crown, 24
  during takeoff run, 26–28
  taxiing, 13
Drift
  departing pattern, 33
  jet-engine blast, 82
  vortices, 81, 82

Electrical master switch
  in-flight malfunction, 18
  over-voltage, 11
  starting engine, 9
Emergency landing, 88–90
  cardinal rule, 126
  at night, 101
Engine malfunction
  engine fire, 8
  hand propping, 7
  starting difficulty, 8, 10
  on takeoff, 87–90
Engine performance
  air temperature, 58
  field elevation, 56–57
  and manifold pressure, 35
  power curve, 54–55
  and proper fuel mixture, 21

use of throttle, 25
verifying output, 25, 65
Engine warm-up, 10–11
Estimating
    abort/stop distance, 67, 74
    crosswind component, 29
    grass-runway takeoff distance, 47–48
    headwind component, 61
    hot-day takeoff distance, 58
    initial climb crosswind correction, 31, 106
    jet-blast separation, 82
    lightly loaded takeoff distance, 62
    obstacle height, 50
    standard-day temperature, 58
    tailwind takeoff distance, 83
    wind velocity, 30, 61

Fail-safe measures
    abort point, 66–67, 74
    minimum safe runway, 66
Field elevation
    fuel mixture, 21–22
    mountain takeoff, 83–85
    takeoff performance, 56
Flaps
    clearing obstacle, 65–66
    preflight check, 23
    retraction, 33, 65–66
    for soft-field takeoff, 74
    stall hazard, 33, 65–66
    takeoff position, 23
Flashlight, 103, 104
Flying, basic truth of, 124
Fuel gauge
    minimum safe indication, 6
    noting departure time, 16
    preflight inspection and check, 18
Fuel mixture
    and carburetor heat, 6, 22
    engine starting, 8
    high-altitude airport, 21–22
    overrich, 6, 21, 22
    takeoff, 21–22

Fuel-tank selector, 6, 21
Fuse replacement, 104–5

Gear-up malfunction, 6
Ground effect, 73–74
Ground run
    acceleration and, 25–26
    aircraft loading, 62
    crosswind correction, 28–29
    directional control, 26–28
    headwind shortens, 60
    tailwind takeoffs, 83–84
Ground speed
    ground-run acceleration, 25, 56
    during taxi, 13, 74–75
    time toward obstacle, 57–58, 84
Gyroscopic precession, 114. See also Torque

Hand propping, 7
Heading indicator
    at night, 97, 107
    preflight check, 17
Headwind
    climb time and distance, 60
    estimating component, 61
    estimating velocity, 61
    shortens ground run, 60
High altitude
    expected environment, 84
    leaning mixture, 21–22
    reduced performance, 56
    simulating performance, 84–85

"Immediate takeoff," 24
In-flight discrepancy
    alternator, 18
    engine malfunction, 87–90
    open door, 85–87
In-flight illusions, 96–97
Instructor, need for
    mountain takeoffs, 85
    recurrent training, 125

Instructor, need for (*cont.*)
  short-field technique, 64
  tailwheel airplane, 111–12
Instrument capability
  at night, 98
  FAA experiment, 106
  testing for, 98–99
Instruments
  at night, 98, 106–7
  preflight checks, 16–19

Jet blast
  in run-up area, 15, 82–83
  minimum separation, 82
Jurisdiction, ground control, 23

Landing gear
  down and locked, 6
  retracting, 33
  and soft fields, 71–72
  tailwheel characteristics, 71, 112–15
Leaving the pattern, 35
Leveling to cruise, 36
  checklist, 43

Magnetic compass, 17
Magnetos
  fast kill, 9
  preflight check, 22
  starting engine, 10
Manufacturer's recommendations
  (airplane manual)
  best angle of climb, 52
  best rate of climb, 54
  cardinal rule, 123–24
  climb speed, 35
  flap position, 51
  fuel pump to prime (start), 8
  fuel-tank selection, 21
  magneto start position, 10
  manual possession, 31
  maximum crosswind component, 29
  preflight research, 64
  rotate speed, 31, 52

starting mixture, 8
starting throttle setting, 8
tire inflation, 48
trim-tab position, 20
Minimum safe fuel, 6
Mixture control
  cruise fuel flow, 37
  high-altitude takeoff, 21–22
  starting engine, 8
Mountain airport
  aircraft performance, 56
  fuel mixture, 21
  pilot experience, 84
  simulation, 85
  and temperature, 58
  verifying engine performance, 65
Mountain takeoff, simulating, 85
Mountain turbulence, 84

Night takeoff
  hazards, 95–102
  instrument ability, 98
  in mountains, 84
  pilot technique, 103–7
  radar services, 103
  weather briefing, 99
Night vision
  and clean windscreen, 105
  evaluating weather, 99, 100
  reduced visibility, 100–1

Oil pressure
  starting engine, 11
  before takeoff, 18
Oil-pressure gauge
  cold-weather starts, 11
  preflight check, 11, 18
Oil temperature
  and operating power, 11
  preflight check, 18

Pattern departure, 35
P factor. *See also* Torque

at lift-off, 31–32
tailwheel aircraft, 114
Pilot ability
  cardinal rule, 124
  "immediate takeoff," 24
  mountain airport, 84
  night takeoff, 98
  practice, 125
  as team member, 124
Pilot technique
  mountain airport, 83–85
  night departure, 103–7
  short-field, 64–66
  soft-field, 74–75
Power settings
  during altitude change, 35
  climb, 35
  full-power run-up, 64
  leveling to cruise, 36
  maximum taxi, 75
  mountain leaning, 22
  starting engine, 8
  warm-up, 11
Preflight inspection, cardinal rule, 122
Preflight planning charts
  aircraft data, 121
  crosswind component, 29
  headwind component, 61
  short-field, 69
Preflight research, 64
  Airport/Facility Directory, 84
  crosswind component, 29–30
  determining runway temperature, 58
  headwind component, 60–61
  mountain airport, 84
  performance charts, 47, 84, 124
  pilot skill, 98, 124
  radio frequencies, 103–4, 109
  short-field research, 47, 69
  unfamiliar aircraft, 31, 121
  weather, 84, 99
  weight and balance, 64
Pretakeoff checks, soft-field, 74
Priming engine, 8
Propwash
  in run-up area, 14

slipstream effect, 26
starting engine, 8
wake turbulence, 79
Propeller
  engine start, 7
  hand propping, 7
  P factor, 31, 114
  preflight check, 23
  soft-field precaution, 75
  takeoff pitch, 23
Propeller area
  clearing, 8–9
  emergency shutdown, 9
  at night, 105
  "stuck" airplane, 75

Radar service
  on departure, 34
  at night, 103
Reduced engine output, 57
  and fuel mixture, 57
  at high elevations, 56
  runway temperature, 58
  simulating mountain takeoff, 85
Reduced lift, 56
Region of reverse command, 54–55.
  See also Backside of power curve
Rotate speed
  mountain airport, 57
  short-field, 52
  soft-field, 74
Runway distance
  cardinal rule, 125
  minimum safe, 66
  tailwind takeoff, 83
  using all of, 65
Runway gradient, 83
Runway surface conditions, 47
  estimating extra distance, 47
  runway gradient, 83
  soft-field, 48
  taxiing, 74
  tire pressure, 48
Runway temperature
  determining, 58

Runway temperature (*cont.*)
  mountain airport, 58

S-turns
  taxiing tailwheelers, 112
  traffic avoidance, 35
Seat belt and harness
  children and FARs, 20
  instructing passengers, 5
  turbulence intensity and, 102
Seat of pants, 115
Seat position, 5
Short-field takeoff
  abort/stop planning, 66–67
  fail-safe measures, 66–67
  hazards of stalling, 52–54
  minimum safe runway length, 66
Slipstream effect. *See also* Torque
  tailwheel aircraft, 114
  on takeoff run, 26–27
Soft-field takeoff
  ground effect, 73–74
  and landing gear, 71
  pilot technique, 74–75
Standard-day temperature, 58
Starting engine, 4–12
  at night, 105
  near FBO, 9

Tachometer
  early in takeoff run, 25
  preflight check, 18–19
Tailwheel rigging, simulating, 72–73
Tailwheel takeoff
  center of gravity, 112, 115
  gyroscopic precession, 114
  takeoff run, 112–14
  taxiing, 112
Takeoff performance charts
  best angle of climb speed, 54–56, 57
  best rate of climb speed, 52–54
  cardinal rule, 124
  flaps, 51
  gross weight, 62
  ground run, 49

headwind component, 60–61
  pilot technique, 64
  rotate speed, 52, 57
  runway surface, 47
  runway temperature, 58–59
  total to clear obstacle, 49–51
  use of, 84, 124
Takeoff variables, 47–66
  mountain airports, 83
Taking the runway, 24–25
  at soft field, 75
Taxiing
  braking, 13, 14
  cardinal rule, 126
  cowl flaps, 6
  crosswind correction, 13
  defensive taxiing, 12
  high-power taxi, 65, 75
  jet-blast avoidance, 82
  at night, 105
  smoothness, 12–14
  soft-field operations, 74–75
  speed, 13, 74–75
  steering, 13
Temperature, 58
Throttle
  best accelerations, 25
  engine warm-up, 10–11
  starting position, 8
Tire inflation, 48
Torque, 33. *See also* P factor;
    Gyroscopic precession; Slipstream
    effect
  during initial climb, 26
  leveling to cruise, 37
Total awareness
  defined, xi-xii
  using, 127
Total distance to clear obstacle, 49–51
  soft-field calculation, 74
Traffic avoidance
  airport traffic area, 34
  to cruise altitude, 35–36
  departing uncontrolled airport, 24
  during initial climb, 33–34
  radar services, 34, 103
  taxiing, 12

Traffic pattern
  departure, 35
  locating emergency fields, 89, 126
Trim tab
  during flap retraction, 33
  during initial climb, 33
  leveling to cruise, 37
  out-of-trim hazards, 20
  preflight check, 20
Turbulence
  intensities,102–3
  in mountains, 84
  at night, 102
  wake, 79–83
Turn indicator, preflight check, 17

Vertical speed indicator

at night, 96, 106
  preflight check, 17
Vortices
  avoiding, 81–83
  behavior of, 80–81
  and ground effect, 73

Wake turbulence. *See* Vortices
Wind drift. *See also* Crosswind
  correction
  jet blast, 82
  leaving pattern, 33
  at night, 102
  wing-tip vortices, 81
Windows and doors
  open door, 85–87
  preflight check, 21